Grammar and punctuation

Teacher's Resource Book

TERMS AND CONDITIONS

IMPORTANT – PERMITTED USE AND WARNINGS – READ CAREFULLY BEFORE USING

This CD-ROM has been tested for viruses at all stages of its production. However, we recommend that you run virus-checking software on your computer systems at all times. Scholastic Ltd cannot accept any responsibility for any loss, disruption or damage to your data or your computer system that may occur as a result of using either the CD-ROM or the data held on it.

IF YOU ACCEPT THE ABOVE CONDITIONS YOU MAY PROCEED TO USE THE CD-ROM.

Recommended system requirements:

Windows: XP (Service Pack 3), Vista (Service Pack 2), Windows 7 or Windows 8 with 2.33GHz processor
Mac: OS 10.6 to 10.8 with Intel Core™ Duo processor
1GB RAM (recommended)
1024 x 768 Screen resolution
CD-ROM drive (24x speed recommended)
Adobe Reader (version 9 recommended for Mac users)
Broadband internet connections (for installation and updates)

For all technical support queries (including no CD drive), please phone Scholastic Customer Services on 0845 6039091.

Authors
Leonie Bennett and Lesley Fletcher

Editorial team
Rachel Morgan, Melissa Somers, Red Door Media, Gemma Cary and Margaret Eaton

Series designers
Shelley Best and Anna Oliwa

Design team
Nicolle Thomas and Neil Salt

Illustrations
Garry Davies and Frazer Worth

CD-ROM development
Hannah Barnett, Phil Crothers and MWA Technologies Private Ltd

Designed using Adobe Indesign
Published by Scholastic Ltd,
Book End, Range Road, Witney,
Oxfordshire OX29 0YD
www.scholastic.co.uk

Printed by Ashford Colour Press

1 2 3 4 5 6 7 8 9 5 6 7 8 9 0 1 2 3 4

British Library Cataloguing-in-Publication Data
A catalogue record for this book is available from the British Library.
ISBN 978-1407-14065-0

Contents

Introduction

Scholastic English Skills: Grammar and punctuation

This series is based on the premise that grammar and punctuation can be interesting and dynamic – but on one condition. The condition is that the teaching of these grammar aspects must be related to real texts and practical activities that experiment with language, investigate the use of language in realistic contexts and find the ways in which grammar and punctuation are used in our day-to-day speech, writing and reading. This book encourages children to look back at their written work and find ways to revise and improve it.

Teaching grammar and punctuation

'As a writer I know that I must select studiously the nouns, pronouns, verbs, adverbs, etcetera, and by a careful syntactical arrangement make readers laugh, reflect or riot.'

Maya Angelou

The *Scholastic English Skills: Grammar and punctuation* series equips teachers with resources and subject training to enable them to teach grammar and punctuation effectively. The focus of the resource is on what is sometimes termed 'sentence-level work', so called because grammar and punctuation primarily involve the construction and understanding of sentences.

Many teachers bring with them a lot of past memories when they approach the teaching of grammar. Some will remember school grammar lessons as the driest of subjects, involving drills and parsing, and will wonder how they can make it exciting for their own class. At the other end of the spectrum, some will have received relatively little formal teaching of grammar at school. In other words, there are teachers who, when asked to teach clause structure or prepositions, feel at a bit of a loss. They are being asked expectantly to teach things they are not confident with themselves.

Grammar can evoke lethargy, fear, irritation, pedantry and despondency. Yet as demonstrated by the above comment from Maya Angelou, even one of our greatest modern writers presents her crafting of sentences as an exciting and tactical process that has a powerful effect on her readers. Can this be the grammar that makes teachers squirm or run?

About the product

The book is divided into six chapters. Each chapter looks at a different aspect of grammar and punctuation and is divided into sections. Each section includes teachers' notes – objective, background knowledge, notes on how to use the photocopiable pages, further ideas and digital content – and three photocopiable pages.

Posters

Each chapter has two posters. These posters are related to the contents of the chapter and should be displayed and used for reference throughout the work on the chapter. The poster notes (on the chapter introduction page) offer suggestions for how they could be used. There are black and white versions in the book and full-colour versions on the CD-ROM for you to print out or display on your whiteboard.

Activities

Each section contains three activities. These activities all take the form of a photocopiable page which is in the book. Each photocopiable page is also included on the CD-ROM for you to display or print out (answers are also provided, where appropriate, in a separate document on the CD-ROM).

Many of the photocopiable pages have linked interactive activities on the CD-ROM. These interactive activities are designed to act as starter activities to the lesson, giving whole-class support on the information being taught. However, they can also work equally well as plenary activities, reviewing the work the children have just completed.

Workbooks

Accompanying this series is a set of workbooks containing practice activities which are divided into chapters to match the teacher's resource book. Use a combination of the photocopiable pages in this book and the activities in the workbook to help children practise and consolidate grammar and punctuation skills.

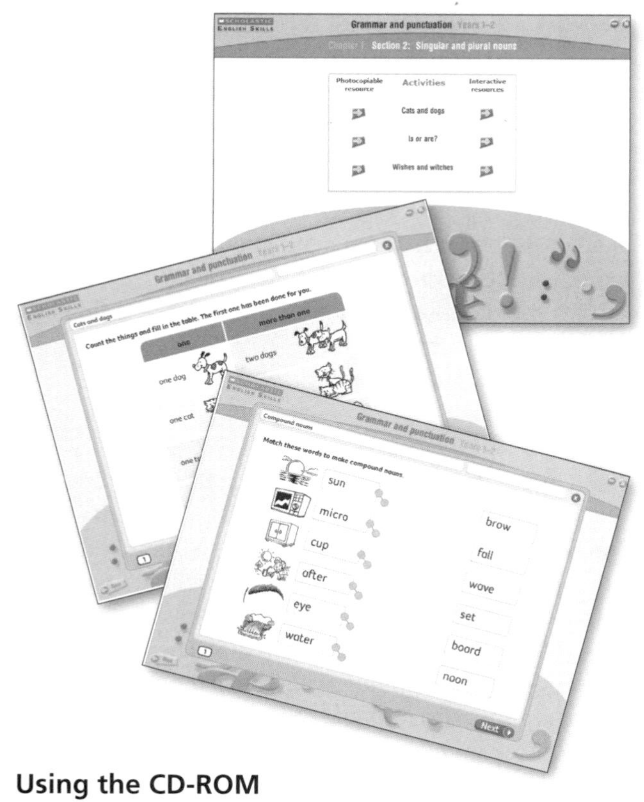

Using the CD-ROM

Below are brief guidance notes for using the CD-ROM. For more detailed information, see 'How to use this digital content' on the Main menu.

The CD-ROM follows the structure of the book and contains:

- All of the photocopiable pages.
- All of the poster pages in full colour.
- Answers provided, where relevant.
- Interactive on-screen activities linked to the photocopiable pages.

Getting started

Put the CD-ROM into your CD-ROM drive.

- For Windows users, the install wizard should autorun, if it fails to do so then navigate to your CD-ROM drive. Then follow the installation process.
- For Mac users, copy the disk image file to your hard drive. After it has finished copying double click it to mount the disk image. Navigate to the mounted disk image and run the installer. After installation the disk image can be unmounted and the DMG can be deleted from the hard drive.
- To install on a network, please see the ReadMe file located on the CD-ROM (navigate to your drive).

To complete the installation of the program you need to open the program and click 'Update' in the pop-up. Please note – this CD-ROM is web-enabled and the content will be downloaded from the internet to your hard-drive to populate the CD-ROM with the relevant resources. This only needs to be done on first use, after this you will be able to use the CD-ROM without an internet connection. If at any point any content is updated you will receive another pop-up upon start up with an internet connection.

Main menu

The main menu is the first screen that appears. Here you can access: terms and conditions, registration links, how to use the CD-ROM and credits. To access a specific year group click on the relevant button (NB only titles installed will be available). To browse all installed content click **All resources**.

Chapter menu

The Chapter menu provides links to all of the chapters or all of the resources for a specific year group. Clicking on the relevant Chapter icon will take you to the section screen where you can access the posters and the chapter's sections. Clicking on **All resources** will take you to a list of all the resources, where you can search by keyword or chapter for a specific resource.

Section menu

Here you can choose the relevant section to take you to its activity screen. You can also access the posters here.

Activity menu

Upon choosing a section from the section menu, you are taken to a list of resources for that section. Here you can access all of the photocopiable pages related to that section as well as the linked interactive activities.

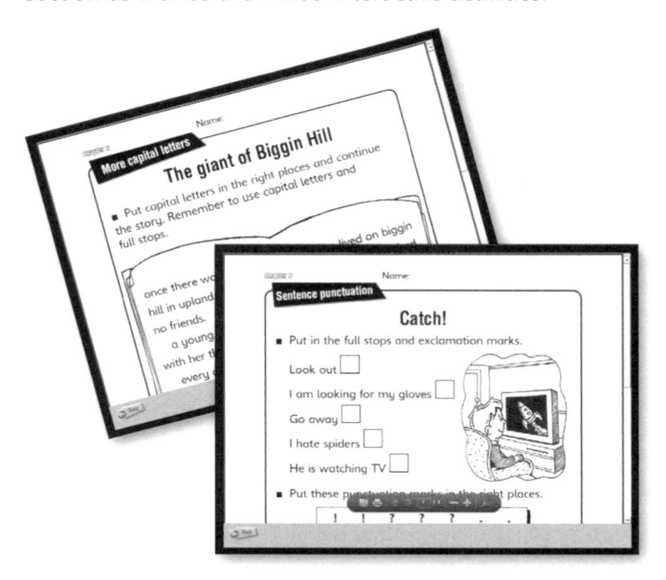

All resources

All of the resources for a year group (if accessed via a Chapter menu) or all of the installed resources (if accessed via the Main menu). You can:

- Select a chapter and/or section by selecting the appropriate title from the drop-down menus.
- Search for key words by typing them into the search box.
- Scroll up or down the list of resources to locate the required resource.
- To launch a resource, simply click on the **Go** button.

Navigation

The resources (poster pages, photocopiable pages and interactive activities) all open in separate windows on top of the menu screen. To close a resource, click on the **x** in the top right-hand corner of the screen and this will return you to the menu screen.

Closing a resource will not close the program. However, if you are in a menu screen, then clicking on the **x** will close the program. To return to a previous menu screen, you need to click on the **Back** button.

Teacher settings

In the top left-hand corner of the Main menu screen is a small **T** icon. This is the teacher settings area. It is password protected, the password is: login. This area will allow you to choose the print quality settings for interactive activities 'Default' or 'Best'. It will also allow you to check for updates to the program or re-download all content to the disk via **Refresh all content**.

Answers

The answers to the photocopiable pages can be found on the CD-ROM in the All resources menu. The answers are supplied in one document in a table-format, referencing the page number, title and answer for each relevant page. The pages that have answers are referenced in the 'Digital content' boxes on the teachers' notes pages. Unfortunately, due to the nature of English, not all pages can have answers provided because some activities require the children's own imaginative input or consist of a wider writing task.

Objectives

	Page	Section	English skills objective	Year 1 To use regular plural noun suffixes 's' or 'es'.	Year 1 To add suffixes to verbs when no change of the root word is needed.	Year 1 To use the prefix 'un' to change the meaning of verbs and adjectives.	Year 1 To use a capital letter for the names of people, places, the days of the week, and the personal pronoun 'I'.	Year 2 To form nouns using suffixes such as 'ness' or 'er' and by compounding.	Year 2 To form adjectives using suffixes such as 'ful' and 'less'.	Year 2 To use the suffixes 'er' and 'est' to form adjectives and 'ly' to turn adjectives into adverbs.	Year 2 To make the correct choice and consistent use of present tense and past tense throughout writing.	Year 2 To use the progressive form of verbs in the present and past tense to mark actions in progress.
Chapter 1	12	Nouns	Recognise and classify nouns.	✓				✓				
	16	Singular and plural nouns	Identify singular and plural nouns and use them in sentences.	✓								
	20	Proper nouns	Recognise proper nouns and begin them with capital letters.				✓					
	24	Forming nouns	Understand how nouns can be formed.					✓				
	28	Writing with nouns	Use nouns appropriately in writing.				✓					
Chapter 2	35	What is an adjective?	Recognise and understand the function of adjectives.			✓				✓		
	39	Using adjectives	Use a variety of adjectives.			✓			✓	✓		
	43	Playing with adjectives	Understand how adjectives can be changed and formed using prefixes and suffixes.			✓			✓	✓		
	47	Using 'er' and 'est'	Use the suffixes 'er' and 'est' in adjectives.							✓		
	51	Adverbs	Recognise and understand the function of adverbs.							✓		
	55	Writing with adjectives	Write effectively for purpose using adjectives.			✓			✓	✓		
Chapter 3	62	What is a verb?	Recognise and understand the function of verbs in sentences.			✓						
	66	Verbs – present and past tense (1)	Use the present and past tenses correctly.		✓						✓	
	70	Verbs – present and past tense (2)	Use the present and past tenses correctly and consistently.		✓						✓	
	74	Verbs – action in progress	Use the progressive form of verbs in the present and past tense to mark actions in progress.		✓							✓
	78	Verbs in writing	Use verb tenses correctly and consistently in writing.		✓						✓	

Objectives

	Page	Section	English skills objective	Year 1 To understand how words can combine to make sentences.	Year 1 To join words and sentences using 'and'.	Year 1 To sequence sentences to form short narratives	Year 1 To use a capital letter for the names of people, places, the days of the week, and the personal pronoun 'I'.	Years 1–2 To [begin to] punctuate sentences using capital letters, full stops, question marks or exclamation mark.	Year 2 To use subordination (when, if, that, because) and coordination (or, and, but).	Year 2 To use expanded noun phrases for description and specification	Year 2 To understand how the grammatical patterns in a sentence indicate its function as a statement, question, exclamation or command.	Year 2 To use commas to separate items in lists.	Year 2 To use apostrophe to mark where letters are missing and to mark singular possession in nouns.
Chapter 4	85	What is a sentence?	Recognise and identify the features of a sentence.	✓				✓					
	89	Making sense	Understand that a sentence should make sense and stand alone.	✓				✓					
	93	Using 'and' or 'but'	Join words and join clauses using 'and' or 'but'.		✓				✓				
	97	Asking questions	Identify and compose questions.					✓			✓		
	101	Writing and using sentences	Write and sequence sentences to form short narratives	✓	✓	✓			✓		✓		
Chapter 5	108	Linking words and phrases (1)	Learn how subordinating and coordinating conjunctions can link words and phrases.		✓				✓				
	112	Linking words and phrases (2)	Learn to use subordinating and coordinating conjunction						✓				
	116	Different kinds of sentence	Understand and distinguish between the different functions of sentences.								✓		
	120	Improving your writing	Learn how to use expanded noun phrases.							✓			
	124	Different types of writing	Write for different purposes.			✓		✓		✓	✓		
Chapter 6	131	Sentence punctuation	Begin to punctuate sentences using a capital letter and a full stop, question mark or exclamation mark.					✓					
	135	Using sentence punctuation	Use familiar punctuation correctly.					✓					
	139	More capital letters	Use a capital letter for names of people, places, the days of the week and the personal pronoun.				✓	✓					
	143	Commas in lists	Use commas to separate items in a list.									✓	
	147	Apostrophes for missing letters	Use apostrophes for contracted forms.										✓
	151	Apostrophes for belonging	Use apostrophes to mark singular possession in nouns.										✓

Chapter 1

Nouns

Introduction

This chapter focuses on nouns. It begins by looking at common nouns and then moves on to the names of places, people, days of the week and months of the year, all of which begin with capital letters. Many early years classes refer to nouns as 'naming words'. You should introduce the term 'noun' during Year 2. For further practice, please see the 'Nouns' section of the Years 1–2 workbook.

Poster notes

One or more than one? (page 10)
The poster shows how plurals are made. Explain to the children that most nouns simply have an 's' added, but that there are exceptions. Suggest that the children say a noun with the word 'one' before it, and then say it with the word 'two' before it, listening carefully to the ending. This will give them a clue to words that take 'es' spellings.

Making new nouns (page 11)
The poster shows how compound nouns are made. Explain to the children that compound nouns are two shorter words joined together to make a new one. Invite children to read the first and then the second noun and finally to read the compound noun. New nouns can also be made by adding a suffix to a word. Invite children to read the words and then the suffix, and then to read the new noun made by joining them. Discuss how the meaning has changed.

In this chapter

Vocabulary

In Year 1 children need to know:
word, naming word, doing word, singular, plural

In Year 2 children need to know:
noun, compound, suffix

Nouns

One or more than one?

One (singular)	**More than one** (plural)	**Usual rule**
one cat	two cats  	most words: add **s**
one bus one brush one watch	two buses two brushes  two watches	words ending in **s**, **sh**, **tch** or **x**: add **es**
one fairy 	two fairies 	words ending in **y**: change **y** to **i** and add **es**

Nouns

Making new nouns

- Adding two nouns to make a new noun

First noun	Second noun	Compound noun
car 	pet 	carpet 
foot 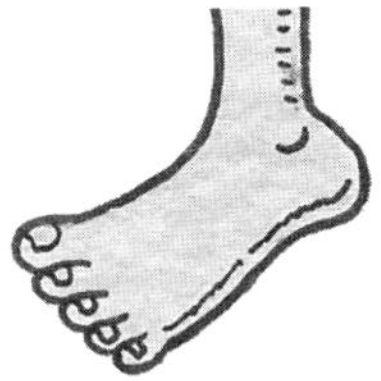	ball 	football 
bed 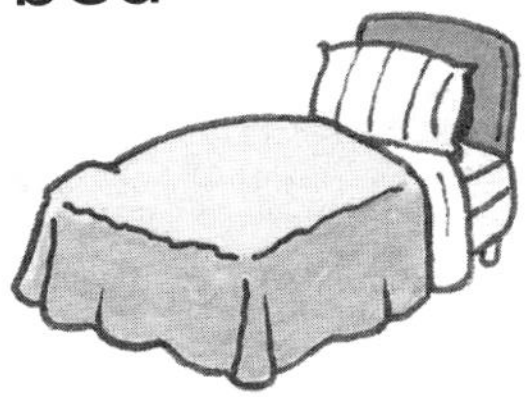	room 	bedroom 

- Adding suffixes to make new nouns

Word	Suffix	New noun
good	ness	goodness 
bad	ness	badness 
teach	er	teacher 
sing	er	singer 

Nouns

Objective

Recognise and classify nouns.

Background knowledge

There are four types of noun:

- **Common nouns:** are the names of things or feelings and refer to any example of the type, for instance 'book' or 'girl'.
- **Proper nouns:** always begin with a capital letter. They are 'special' names that identify a specific place or person, such as 'Sanjay' or 'Glasgow'; or the day of the week or the month of the year.
- **Collective nouns:** refer to a group of things, such as a 'crowd of people'.
- **Abstract nouns:** refer to non-concrete things such as 'happiness' or 'idea'.

Children need to identify 'naming words' and understand that they can be categorised in different ways. You can provide lots of practice orally, focusing on things in the classroom, before moving on to the photocopiable sheets.

Activities

- **Photocopiable page 13 'At home'**

The children should understand that many nouns can be categorised according to where we find them, for example: inside or outside, at the swimming pool, in the park, at the beach and so on. You can talk about the different environments within their homes and ask the children what sort of things they might see there.

- **Photocopiable page 14 'Out and about'**

As for the previous activity, talk briefly about the three environments on the sheet. Tell the children to list as many things as they can that belong in these places. Emphasise that you want them to make a list, so they should just write out the nouns or naming words and not try to put them into sentences.

- **Photocopiable page 15 'What is it? (1)'**

Remind the children how to write lists and explore the idea that nouns or naming words can be collected into groups of type, for example: toys, food, things to write with and so on. Write some of these headings on the board and ask the children to help you to list some nouns that fall into these categories. Next, tell the children to sort the muddled things in the star on the photocopiable sheet into the four lists. They may also be able to think of some extra things. Make sure they all know the meaning of the word 'furniture'.

Further ideas

- **Categories:** Working in groups, ask children to look through magazines or catalogues, finding and cutting out pictures of things that can be categorised, for example: animals, food or toys. Invite them to then stick the pictures on to large sheets of paper, with the category title as a heading and individual naming words next to each picture.

Digital content

On the digital component you will find:

- Printable versions of all three photocopiable pages.
- Answers to 'What is it? (1)'.
- Interactive versions of 'At home' and 'What is it? (1)'.

Name:

Nouns

At home

■ List some things you would see in these places.

In the kitchen	In the bedroom	In the lounge

Name:

Out and about

■ List some things you would see in these places.

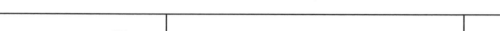

At school 	In the street 	In the park 

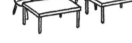

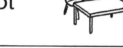

Name:

Nouns

What is it? (1)

■ Sort these nouns into groups. Think of some more nouns to add.

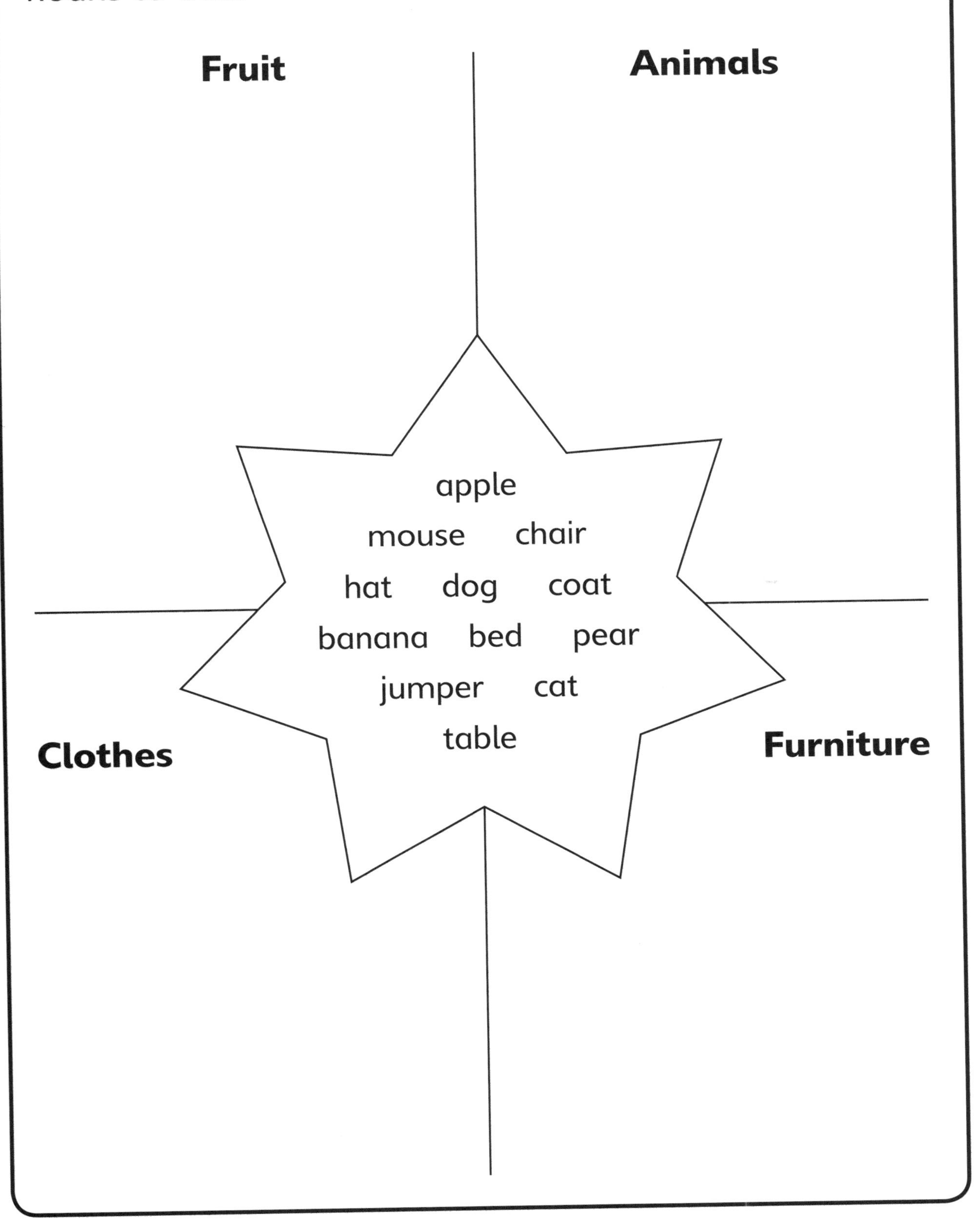

Singular and plural nouns

Objective

Identify singular and plural nouns and use them in sentences.

Background knowledge

Most nouns change their form to indicate quantity by having 's' or 'es' added. But there are other nouns that form the plural by changing the last letter before having 's' added. Words ending in 'y' form the plural by having the 'y' deleted and 'ies' added. Some words ending in 'f' form the plural by having 'f' deleted and 'ves' added. Other nouns form the plural irregularly, for example: *man–men; child–children*. Children need to learn the general rule of adding 's' to indicate a plural noun. Through practice they will learn to recognise the exceptions. Children will also become aware that changing singular to plural results in other words changing to agree with the noun.

Activities

- **Photocopiable page 17 'Cats and dogs'**

Read the left-hand column with the children (*one dog* and so on), then look at the illustrations in the right-hand column. Invite the children to tell you how many dogs, cats, trees and ducks there are in each. Look at the sample answer and point out the 's' on the end of 'dogs', pointing out that this tells us that there is more than one dog. Explain to the children that 'dog' is the singular form of the noun and that 'dogs' is the plural form of the noun. Ask them to count the other things and write the correct numbers and naming words that correspond to the illustrations. Children can then write their own sentence about the picture.

- **Photocopiable page 18 'Wishes and witches'**

Ask children to suggest some nouns that form the plural by having 'es' added. Alternatively, give them some singular nouns and ask them which they would add 's' to and which they would add 'es' to. Ask children to complete the activity by writing the word 'two' followed by the plural form of the noun. They can then use the plurals to complete the sentences below. Remind children to leave a space between each word. Finally, invite them to write their own sentence on the back of the sheet using 'wishes' and 'witches'. They may wish to discuss with a partner what kind of sentence might include these two words.

- **Photocopiable page 19 'Is or are?'**

Make a simple sentence using a singular noun (naming word). For example: *My brother is funny.* Then say the sentence using the plural: *My brothers are funny.* Ask children what else has changed in the sentence apart from the noun (the verb or doing word). Practise changing other sentences from singular to plural. Ask children to read each of the sentences on the photocopiable sheet and choose between 'is' and 'are'. Invite them to use their own words to complete the last two sentences. Remind children to leave a space between each word. One is in the singular and the other is in the plural.

Further ideas

- **Shared text:** When sharing a text, ask the children to look out for singular and plural nouns.
- **Unusual plurals:** Plurals that add 's' and 'es' to the singular form can be added to a class collection of words that form plurals in different ways for Year 1 children. Also include adding 'ies' to the singular form for Year 2 children.

Digital content

On the digital component you will find:

- Printable versions of all three photocopiable pages.
- Answers to all three photocopiable pages.
- Interactive versions of all three photocopiable pages.

Name:

Singular and plural nouns

Cats and dogs

■ Count the things and fill in the table. The first one has been done for you.

One	More than one
one dog	two dogs
one cat	
one tree	
one duck	

■ Look at the picture below. Write a sentence about this picture on another sheet of paper.

Name:

Singular and plural nouns

Wishes and witches

■ Add **es** to show that there is more than one of each of these things.

one brush 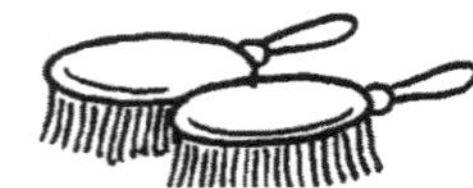 two ______________________

one bus  two ______________________

one wish  ______________________

one potato  ______________________

one kiss   ______________________

one witch  ______________________

one box  ______________________

one class 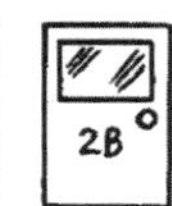

____

■ Use one of the words you have made to finish these sentences.

1. I shut my eyes and made three ______________________ .

2. We had to get two ______________________ to my uncle's house.

3. The computer came in two big ______________________ .

4. Dad cooked lots of ______________________ .

Is or are?

■ Finish these sentences. Circle the correct word at the end of the line and then write it in the space.

1. The girls ____________ happy.	is	are
2. Both boys ____________ seven years old.	is	are
3. The bus ____________ full.	is	are
4. All of these trees ____________ very tall.	is	are
5. My hat ____________ on my head.	is	are
6. My teacher ____________ called Mrs Khan.	is	are

■ Finish these sentences.

1. My teacher ______________________________

____

____.

2. Some children in my class ____________________

____

____.

Proper nouns

Objective

Recognise proper nouns and begin them with capital letters.

Background knowledge

Common nouns are general names for things. For example, in the sentence *I fed the dog*, the noun 'dog' could be used to refer to any dog, not to a specific one. Children should recognise that some nouns are special, and that to show they are special we start them with capital letters. These words – which identify specific things or people – are proper nouns. In a phrase such as *Jess is my dog* the word 'dog' is the common noun; 'Jess' is a proper noun because it refers to and identifies a specific dog.

Activities

- **Photocopiable page 21 'Here I am'**
Point out that 'I' is always a capital letter when it stands alone. The writer, to whom it refers, is very special. Tell the children to draw a picture of themselves and of you on the sheet, and then to finish the sentences. Remind them to use capital letters to begin names and to put a full stop at the end of each sentence. Talk about who they might draw in the last box – perhaps a friend, their mum or a pet. Explain that they should choose either 'She' or 'He' to begin each of the last two sentences.
- **Photocopiable page 22 'Me and my animals'**
Tell the children that they are going to write about themselves and make up names for some animals. They should then write about one of the animals they have named. Remind the children that the names and sentences should reflect the animal characteristics that they are thinking about.
- **Photocopiable page 23 'People and places'**
Read through the sentences on the sheet and ask the children to look for the special words that need capitals. Remind them that a word such as 'cats' (in the last sentence) doesn't require a capital letter because it is not the special name of a particular cat. When they have completed the activity, invite the children to go on to make two lists on another sheet of paper – a list of people and a list of places – starting with those on the sheet, and then adding their own.

Further ideas

- **Shared reading:** In shared reading, point out a character's name and draw attention to the capital letter. Ask the children to find people's names in other texts, displayed on a whiteboard, inviting them to highlight the capital letter each time. Ask them to find and mark other names in different texts.
- **Finding capitals:** Give each group a book to look through for capital letters. Ask them to pick out all the different reasons capital letters are used, and then feed back to the rest of the class with their examples.

Digital content

On the digital component you will find:
- Printable versions of all three photocopiable pages.
- Answers to 'People and places'.
- Interactive version of 'People and places'.

Proper nouns

Here I am

■ Draw pictures in the boxes. Write sentences to go with them. Remember to use capital letters.

Here I am.

My name is ________________ .

This is my teacher.

________ is called ________________ .

He She

This is my ________________

________ is called ________________ .

He She

Name:

Proper nouns

Me and my animals

■ Write about yourself. Remember to use capitals to begin names and places.

My name is ________________________ .

I live in a place called ____________________ .

Two people in my family are ________________

and ________________ .

If I had a dog I would call it ________________ .

If I had a fish I would call it ________________ .

■ Think of names for these animals.

________________ ________________ ________________

■ Choose one of these and write a sentence about it.

____

____

____

Proper nouns

People and places

■ These sentences all begin with capital letters, but other capital letters are missing. Rewrite the sentences, putting all the capital letters in the right places.

1. I went to see aunty suzie.

____

2. I got a postcard from america.

____

3. Did you see joe?

____

4. They are going to london.

____

5. I went to southport last week.

____

6. My teacher is miss dean.

____

7. My uncle tim lives in blackpool.

____

Forming nouns

Objective

Understand how nouns can be formed.

Background knowledge

New nouns can be made by combining two nouns together. If we put 'sun' and 'shine' together, we make the compound noun 'sunshine'. Each part of the word is spelled the same as when it was a separate word. Adding suffixes to words can also create nouns. If we add 'ness' to some words we can make new abstract nouns (though children don't need to be familiar with this term). So 'weak' and 'ness' makes the abstract noun 'weakness'. Adding the suffix 'er' to some words can also make new nouns. 'Paint' and 'er' makes the noun 'painter'. The spelling of the root word has not changed. If you add 'er' to a word ending in 'e', such as 'ride', you need to drop the final 'e' before adding 'er', in this case making 'rider'.

Activities

- **Photocopiable page 25 'Compound nouns'**
Tell the children that by putting two short words together, we can make new words, called 'compound nouns'. As a class, look at the poster 'Making new nouns' (page 11), and ask children to read through the examples. Then show the children the photocopiable sheet. Invite a child to read the example 'sun' + 'set' and discuss how two short words can create a larger word. The spelling of the two words has not changed, but the meaning of the new word is different. Ask the children to join words from each column to make new compound nouns, which they can write in the boxes provided. Challenge them to think of their own words to create compound nouns and to use these in sentences.

- **Photocopiable page 26 'Adding suffixes to make nouns'**
Explain that a suffix is an ending to a word. Invite children to give examples of different word endings, such as 'ed', 'ing', 'ly', 'ness' and 'er'. Tell the children that they are going to use the suffix, 'er' to make new nouns. If a word ends in 'e' they should remove the final 'e' from the word and then add 'er', as in 'mine' and 'miner'.

- **Photocopiable page 27 'Which suffix?'**
Tell the children that there are different suffixes that can be added to nouns to make new words. Show children the photocopiable sheet and introduce them to the suffixes 'ness', 'ment' and 'hood'. Encourage them to suggest words with these endings. Ask them to work through the sheet, creating new words. Discuss the meaning of the new words and invite them to use these words in sentences.

Further ideas

- **Making a list:** While reading different texts, encourage the children to find different compound nouns and suffixes. Create a class list of new compound words and of root words and their suffixes. Encourage them to think of different root words to go with these suffixes.

Digital content

On the digital component you will find:
- Printable versions of all three photocopiable pages.
- Answers to all three photocopiable pages.
- Interactive versions of 'Compound nouns' and 'Adding suffixes to make nouns'.

Forming nouns

Compound nouns

■ Join these words to make compound nouns.
The first one has been done for you.

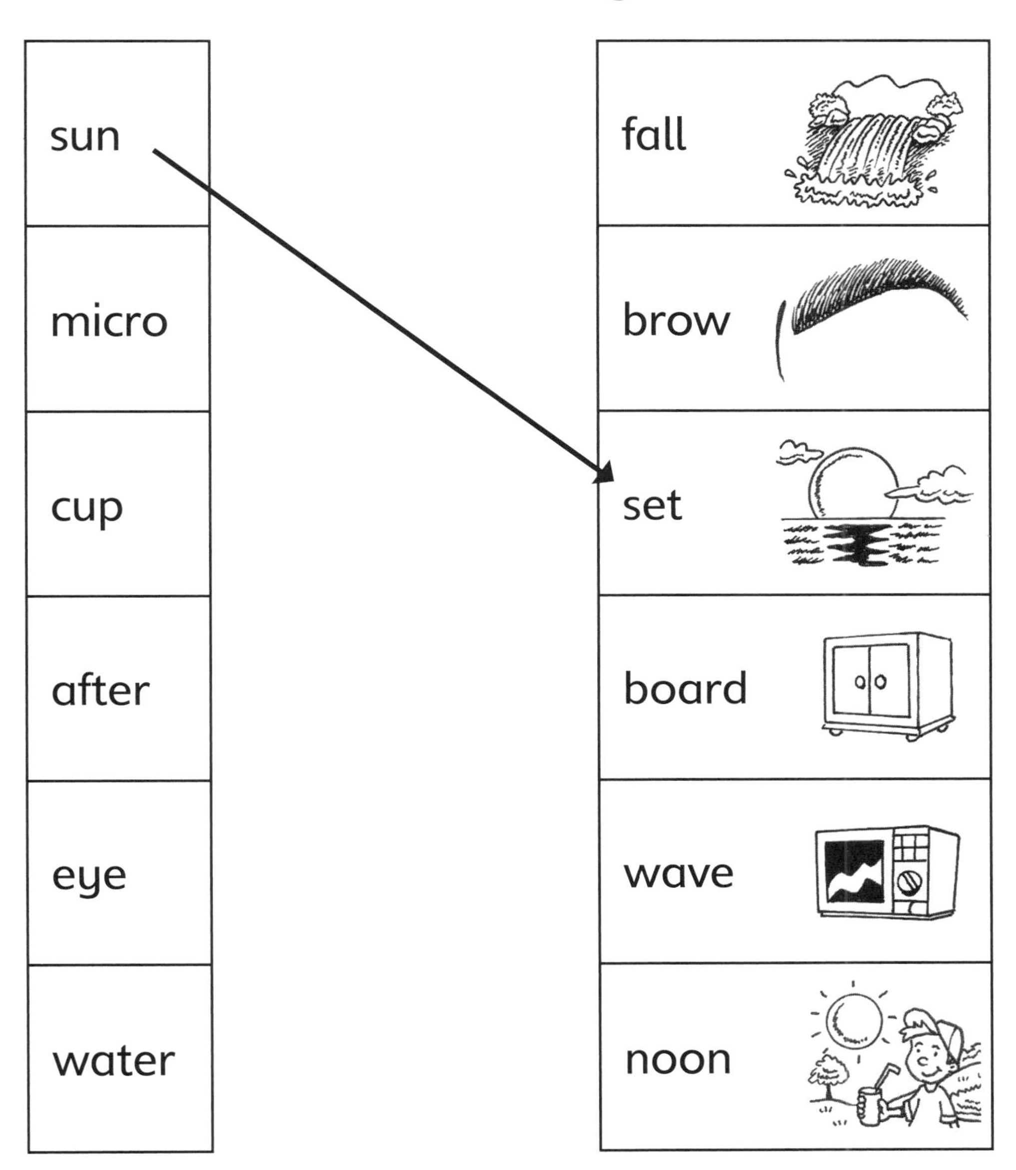

■ Write two words to make your own compound nouns.

_______________ + _______________ = _______________

_______________ + _______________ = _______________

_______________ + _______________ = _______________

Name:

Forming nouns

Adding suffixes to make nouns

■ Add **er** to each word to make a new noun.

teach_______

learn_______

read_______

garden_______

wash_______

■ Rewrite these words and add **er** to them:

hike + **er** = hiker

write _______________

drive _______________

dance _______________

bake _______________

Forming nouns

Which suffix?

■ Choose a suffix (word ending) to make a new noun using the words below.

ness ment hood

child ______

weak ______

cold ______

punish ______

dark ______

■ Write a sentence using one of your words.

______

______

■ Colour the suffixes in this text.

The boy's tidiness pleased his mother. Their relationship was one of agreement and cheerfulness. His childhood had been full of happiness and warmth.

Writing with nouns

Objective

Use nouns appropriately in writing.

Background knowledge

Common and proper nouns have appropriate uses when writing different types of text. Children need to know about different kinds of nouns. Words that name objects, such as *dog* or *cat* are common nouns. Names of people, such as *Michael*, *Maya* and *Mr Chen* are proper nouns. Names of places are proper nouns, such as *England*, *Manchester* and *Blackpool Tower*. Months of the year and days of the week are also proper nouns. All proper nouns begin with a capital letter.

Activities

- **Photocopiable page 29 'In the park with...'**
Ask the children to think of names for the three characters in the activity. Point out that the special names of pets have capital letters, like those of people. The children should write the names again to complete the sentences and then write two sentences of their own about the illustrations. Remind them to use full stops and to leave spaces between words.
- **Photocopiable page 30 'Nursery nouns'**
Read the rhyme with the children. Invite a child to say what a noun (naming word) is. Encourage the children to give examples of several nouns. Re-read the first line, inviting a child to say which word needs underlining. Take suggestions for other nouns to replace it. Explain that the children need to underline all the nouns in the rhyme. They then need to rewrite the rhyme, putting in different nouns. Encourage the children to read their rhymes out to the class.
- **Photocopiable page 31 'Silly sentences (1)'**
Ask the children to give you examples of compound nouns and to tell you which two words made each one. Look at the photocopiable sheet together and invite the children to create different compound nouns using the words in the grid. Challenge the children to make silly sentences using the compound nouns they have discovered. Can they make sentences with two or three compound nouns? Encourage the children to read their sentences to the class at the end of the session.

Further ideas

- **Storing nouns:** When reading different texts, encourage children to find different types of nouns, which they could use in their own writing. Make sure children understand the meaning of new words. Display a collection of interesting nouns that children can refer to when writing.
- **Finding nouns:** When reading stories, encourage children to find and write different types of proper nouns. Make sure children can explain why and where capital letters are used.

Digital content

On the digital component you will find:

- Printable versions of all three photocopiable pages.
- Answers to 'Nursery nouns' and 'Silly sentences (1)'.
- Interactive version of 'Silly sentences (1)'.

Writing with nouns

In the park with...

■ Make up names for these three characters.

■ Complete the sentences. Then finish the story.

Here is ____________________ .

Look at ____________________

and ____________________ .

Name:

Writing with nouns

Nursery nouns

- Underline all the nouns in this rhyme.

Baa, baa, black sheep
Have you any wool?
Yes sir, yes sir,
Three bags full.
One for the master,
One for the dame,
And one for the little boy who lives down the lane.

- Now rewrite it, changing each noun.

Name:

Writing with nouns

Silly sentences (1)

grand sea motor one every
up father hair side
brush stairs bike

■ Use the above words to make compound nouns.

■ Write some silly sentences using these compound nouns.

Chapter 2

Adjectives

Introduction

The aim of this chapter is to enable children to discover the function and explore the variety of adjectives. Children are encouraged to use their creativity to develop their use of adjectives in describing real and imaginary things. They are invited to describe themselves and others and to search for adjectives to use in stories, poems and in persuasive writing. Many early years classes begin by using the term 'describing word' but children will need to move on to using the term 'adjective' in Year 2. For further practice, please see the 'Adjectives' section of the Years 1–2 workbook.

Poster notes

Adjectives (page 33)
This poster provides a range of examples that you can use to introduce the function of adjectives. Show the children some photographs and ask them which of the adjectives from the poster they could use to describe them. Introduce the idea of opposites and help children to find pairs of opposites on the page.

Making adjectives (page 34)
This poster shows children how to make new adjectives by either adding the prefix 'un' or the suffixes 'ful' and 'less'. Explain that adding a word beginning changes each word's meaning. Children are not introduced to the term 'prefix' until Year 3. 'Un' means 'not'. Sometimes adding the prefix 'un' will create verbs as well. Invite children to read through the suffix examples and introduce the term 'suffix' to them, saying that it is a word ending which changes the meaning of the word. Discuss how the suffix has changed each word's meaning.

In this chapter

Vocabulary

In Year 1 children need to know:
describing words, word beginning, word ending

In Year 2 children need to know:
adjective, suffix, adverb

Adjectives
Adjectives
enormous
tiny
friendly
mean
tall
short
loud
quiet
old
young

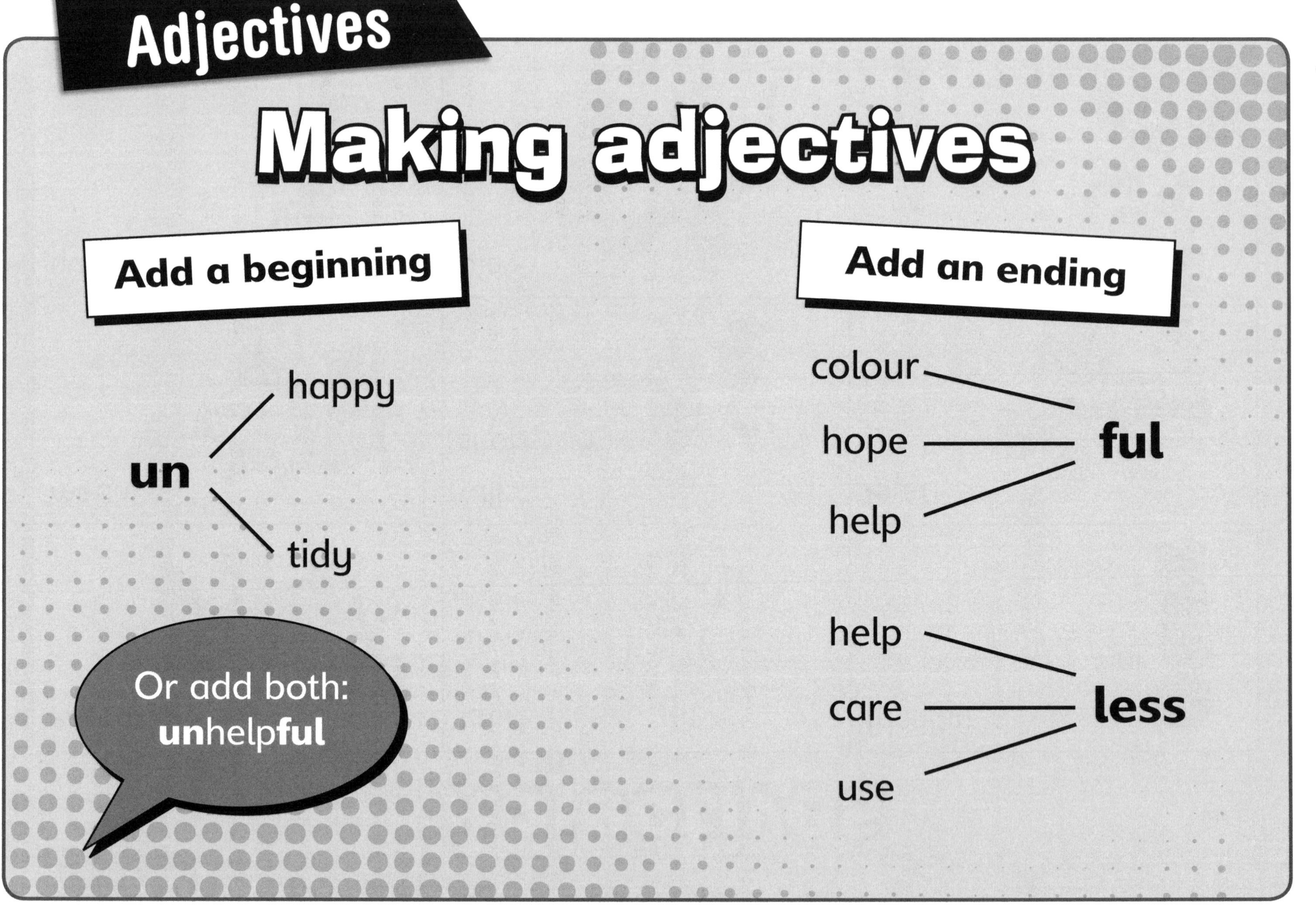
Adjectives
Making adjectives
Add a beginning
un
happy
tidy
Or add both:
unhelpful
Add an ending
colour
hope
help
ful
help
care
use
less

What is an adjective?

Objective

Recognise and understand the function of adjectives.

Background knowledge

Adjectives describe nouns and pronouns – they tell us something about somebody or something. Adjectives come either before a noun, or after a verb – such as 'be', 'get', 'seem' or 'look'. For example: *He is an intelligent boy. That girl is intelligent.* Children should begin to discover the function and explore the variety of adjectives. The phrase 'describing word' can be used until the term 'adjective' is introduced in Year 2.

Find a section of a familiar story that contains several adjectives. Read it to the children, omitting all the adjectives; then read it with the adjectives. Ask the children which passage they prefer and why. Invite them to explain how the passages differ.

Activities

- **Photocopiable page 36 'What's it like? (1)'**
Write a simple sentence on the board, such as: *I have a cat*. Ask the children what they know about your cat from that sentence. Does it tell them what it looks like or how it behaves? Add an adjective, such as 'fluffy', and ask them if that helps and why. Then ask the children to choose one of the words from the box to describe each of the things on the sheet.
- **Photocopiable page 37 'What's it like? (2)'**
Remind the children what they know about describing words. Hold up a classroom object, such as a book, and ask the children to suggest words to describe it. If they say 'red', take the opportunity to point out that colour words are describing words too. Now ask the children to look at the objects in the activity and to think of suitable describing words. They should also draw their own object and describe it, using an adjective and a noun.
- **Photocopiable page 38 'What sort of bike is it?'**
Ask the children to suggest adjectives that could be used to describe a car. Remind them that describing is not limited to what a thing looks like. You can help by asking questions such as: *How old? How fast? How comfortable?* You may take this opportunity to discuss their five senses, by asking what the car sounds like, for example. If they were to touch it, would it be hard or soft? Ask children to think of three adjectives that could be used to describe each of the things on the photocopiable sheet.

Further ideas

- **Alphabetical adjectives:** Choose a noun, such as 'dog' or 'friend', and go round the class asking each child to suggest an adjective, using a different describing word for every letter of the alphabet. So, *My dog is active, My dog is brown, My dog is cute* and so on. You may have to help out with some letters of the alphabet.
- **Think of adjectives:** Alternatively, choose one letter of the alphabet and, as a class, try to find as many adjectives as you can to describe a noun, for example: *My friend is messy, minute, marvellous…*
- **Unusual adjectives:** Encourage the children to think of a variety of adjectives that can be used to describe things that are big, small, nice and not nice (words often overused). Read the following sentences to the children: *My Gran is nice. She has a nice face and she is a very nice person.* Ask them to replace 'nice' with other adjectives and discuss the effect.
- **Shared reading:** During shared reading activities, children can look out for adjectives and try to identify the noun that each one is describing. When reading stories, help children to see where adjectives are used to describe the setting and the characters.

Digital content

On the digital component you will find:
- Printable versions of all three photocopiable pages.
- Answers to 'What's it like (1)'.

Name:

What is an adjective?

What's it like? (1)

- Use a word from the box to describe each picture.

the _______________ hat the _______________ hat

the _______________ car the _______________ car

the _______________ boy the _______________ boy

old	big	sad	new	tiny	happy

Name:

What is an adjective?

What's it like? (2)

- Add a word to describe each of these pictures.
- Draw your own picture and describe it.

the ________________ face

the ________________ man

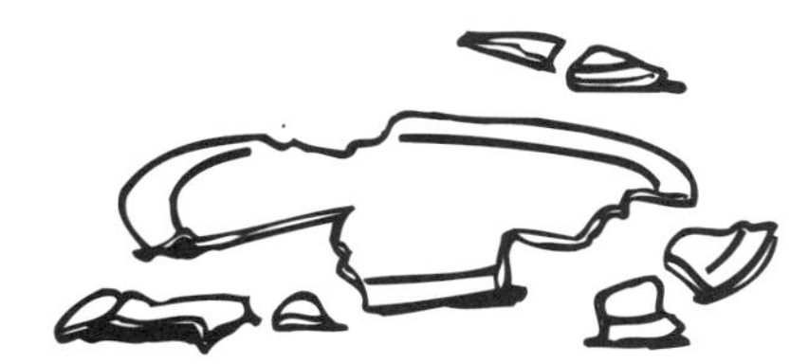

the ________________ plate

the ________________ baby

the ________________ dog

the ______________ monster

the ________________________

____

Name:

What is an adjective?

What sort of bike is it?

■ Think of three adjectives to describe each of these things. Write the words on the lines.

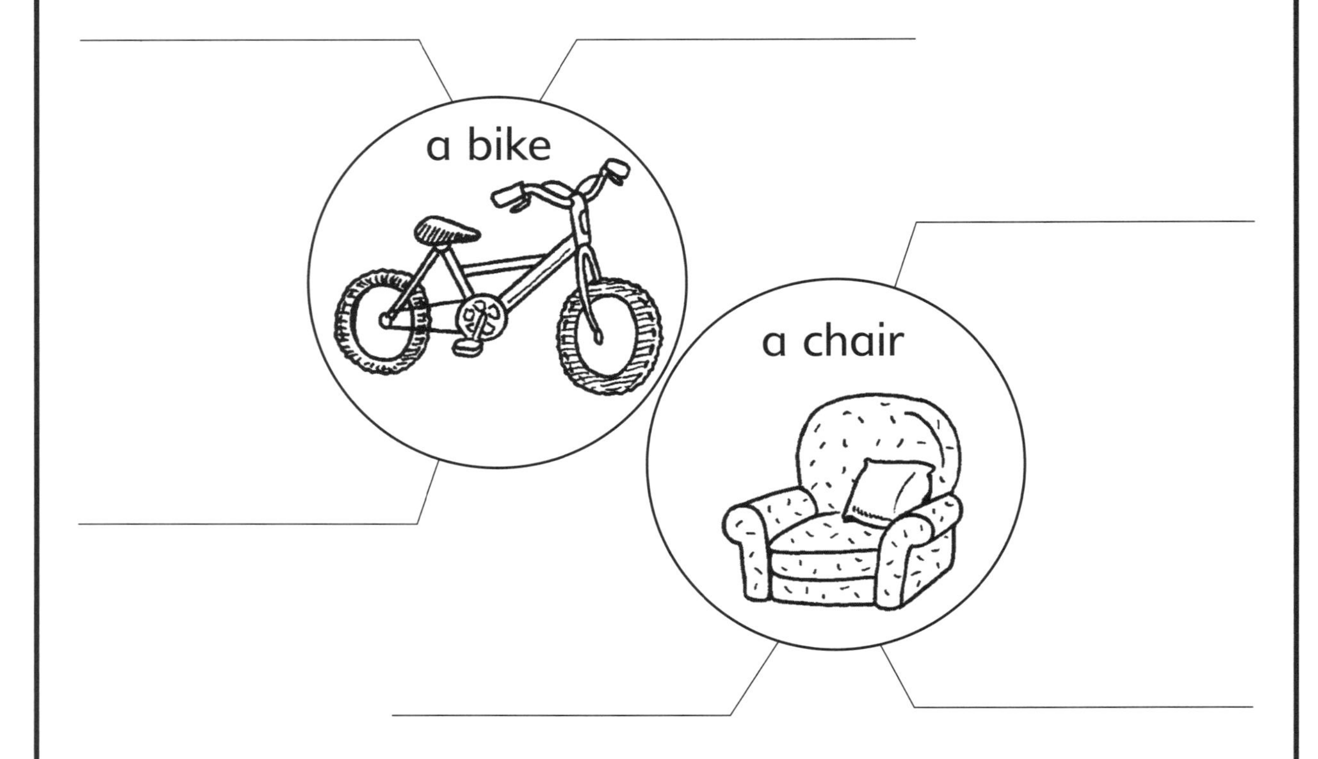

Using adjectives

Objective

Use a variety of adjectives.

Background knowledge

Nouns can be described by more than one adjective: *the very hungry caterpillar* or *ten green bottles*. In some cases, the adjectives must appear in a certain order. For example, you cannot say *green ten bottles* or *the hungry very caterpillar*. Children can have lots of fun exploring adjectives through oral games – changing the adjectives in book or song titles is a good place to start. Encourage them to discuss the effects of their changes. There is a huge range of adjectives and the differences between them can be very subtle. Children should be encouraged to edit their work, trying out different adjectives and considering the different effects, maybe in discussion with their peers.

Activities

- **Photocopiable page 40 'What is red?'**

If possible, read the poem 'What is pink?' by Christina Rossetti to the children. Do the children agree that only oranges are orange? Divide the class into small groups and allocate a colour to each. Ask the groups to make a list of things of their colour before feeding back to the rest of the class. Then ask them to make up their own version of the poem using the photocopiable sheet.

- **Photocopiable page 41 'All about me'**

Tell the children that they are going to explore words they could use to describe themselves. You may like to prepare for this by using the photocopiable sheet as a model to describe yourself and inviting the children's help to complete the activity. Talk through the words at the bottom of the sheet to ensure understanding.

- **Photocopiable page 42 'Tea with a monster'**

Help the children to see that describing words make a story more interesting, and tell them that they have the chance to use some on the sheet. They could work in pairs and discuss whether to describe a good experience (with hot, tasty soup and a soft bed) or a scary experience (with a slimy pudding and a dark, creepy spare bedroom) and should try to think of appropriate adjectives while they are talking. As they complete the photocopiable sheet, encourage them to use two adjectives now and again if they can.

Further ideas

- **Familiar characters:** Look at characters from familiar stories and invite the children to say why they like or dislike them. For example: *I like Snow White because she's kind* or *I don't like the queen because she's wicked.*
- **Adding interest:** Tell the story of 'Goldilocks and the Three Bears' in outline, then invite the children to help you use adjectives to make it more interesting. So, for example: *Goldilocks went for a walk in the woods. She saw a house and went inside. On the table, she saw three bowls of porridge…* could become: *Goldilocks went for a walk in the wild and windy woods near her home. She saw a small green house and went inside. On the rickety wooden table, she saw…*
- **Adjectives in stories:** Invite children to write a story about their visit to the house of a monster. Encourage them to plan a story with the monster's house as the setting. They should describe the problem, the resolution and how they felt using a variety of adjectives.
- **Adjectives in poetry:** Recite the poem 'In a dark, dark wood' to the children. This could be displayed on a whiteboard. Talk about what adjectives other than 'dark' could be used to describe the house, the room and so on, and what might be in the cupboard other than a ghost. Tell children to write their own versions of the poem and share them with the class. Compare the effects of different adjectives.

Digital content

On the digital component you will find:

- Printable versions of all three photocopiable pages.

Name:

Using adjectives

What is red?

■ Complete this poem with your own words.

What is red? A ______________________________ is red.

What is blue? A ______________________________ is blue.

What is brown? A ______________________________ is brown.

What is green? A ______________________________ is green.

What is hard? A ______________________________ is hard.

What is soft? A ______________________________ is soft.

■ Draw a picture to go with your poem.

Using adjectives

All about me

■ What are you like? Use adjectives to describe yourself. You can use some of the words from the bottom of the page.

My hair is ______________ and ______________ .

My eyes are ______________ and ______________ .

My face is ______________ and ______________ .

My hands are ______________ and ______________ .

My feet are ______________ and ______________ .

Sometimes I am ______________ and ______________ .

Sometimes I am ______________ and ______________ .

curly	straight	short	long
square	round	wide	big
thin	small	happy	miserable
cross	funny	kind	rude

Name:

Using adjectives

Tea with a monster

■ Finish this story by adding really interesting adjectives.

A monster invited me for tea.

The soup was ______________________________ .

The pizza was ______________________________ .

The pudding was ______________________________ .

I looked around the monster's house.

The kitchen was ______________________________ .

The spare bedroom was ______________________________ .

The garden was ______________________________ .

I stayed the night.

The bed was ______________________________ .

Next morning, I felt ______________________________ .

Playing with adjectives

Objective

Understand how adjectives can be changed and formed using prefixes and suffixes.

Background knowledge

Adjectives can be created by putting a prefix at the beginning of a word, such as 'un'. Prefixes are word beginnings that change the meaning of the root word, but not its spelling. The prefix 'un' means 'not' and will change the original word to its opposite meaning. So putting 'un' before 'kind' creates a new adjective, 'unkind'. It is also possible to create new verbs using the 'un' prefix. The term 'prefix' is not introduced until Year 3, but you could use the phrase 'word beginning'. Suffixes can also be used to change the meaning of an adjective. The suffix 'ful' means 'full of', so the word 'careful' means 'full of care'. The suffix 'less' means 'without'. So the word 'careless' means 'without care'. The term 'suffix' can be introduced in Year 2.

Activities

- **Photocopiable page 44 'Happy or unhappy?'**

Introduce the prefix 'un'. Explain that some words can have beginnings added to the front to change their meaning. Write the word 'happy' on the board. Ask: *What does this word mean?* Invite a child to write 'un' before the word 'happy' to make 'unhappy'. Ask: *Has the meaning of this word changed?* Explain that putting 'un' before a word changes the first word to its opposite meaning. Ensure the children notice that the spelling of the first word is the same.

Invite the children to practise putting 'un' in front of the words on the photocopiable sheet and to explore the meanings of some 'un' words. Challenge children to think of other words with 'un' at the beginning and to explore their meanings.

- **Photocopiable page 45 'Less or ful?'**

Introduce the suffixes 'less' and 'ful'. Explain that adding a suffix to a root word changes its meaning. Write the word 'hope' on the board. Invite a child to add the suffix 'less' to make 'hopeless'. Ask: *How has this changed its meaning?* Explain that the suffix 'less' means 'without'. Repeat with the suffix 'ful', explaining that 'ful' means 'full of'. Challenge children to add suffixes to the root words provided on the photocopiable sheet and to complete the sentences. Invite the children to read out their sentences, discussing which words make sense and which do not. Ask: *How does using the suffixes 'less' or 'ful' change the meaning of a word or sentence?*

- **Photocopiable page 46 'Fearless suffixes'**

Invite different children to read the opening text. Explain that they should underline all the words with the suffixes 'less' and 'ful'. Ask: *How do these suffixes change the meaning of a root word?* Then ask the children to sort the words they have underlined. Challenge them to work out a rule for adding suffixes to words ending in 'y', before applying the rule to some words. Explain to the children that there are some exceptions to this rule.

Further ideas

- **Put into practice:** Display a list of the prefix and suffix words discovered by the children. Challenge them to use at least three of these in their own writing. Encourage the children to share their sentences and discuss the effectiveness of the new words.

Digital content

On the digital component you will find:

- Printable versions of all three photocopiable pages.
- Answers to 'Happy or unhappy?' and 'Fearless suffixes'.
- Interactive versions of all three photocopiable pages.

Name:

Playing with adjectives

Happy or unhappy?

happy

unhappy

■ Put **un** at the beginning of these words to make new words.

Old word	New word
kind	
happy	
real	
tidy	

■ Match these words to their meanings.

Word	**Meaning**
unused	dangerous
unsafe	hidden
unseen	unfortunate
unlucky	new

■ Use a word starting with **un** in a sentence.

Playing with adjectives

Less or ful?

■ Match each word to an ending to make a new word.

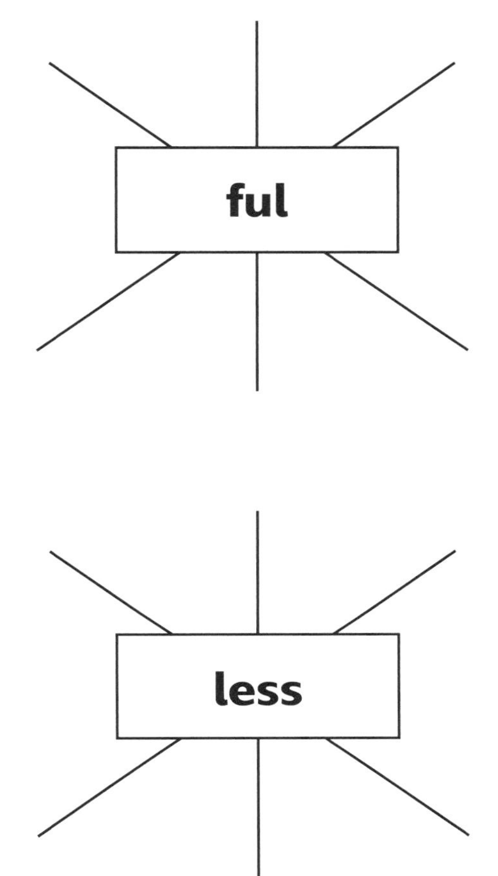

Root word
care
hope
power
tune
help
fear
use
wonder
force
shame

■ Use some of your new words to finish these sentences.

1. Jack's ______________ climbing impressed everyone.

2. Sophie's ______________ writing was difficult to read.

3. They all admired the ______________ view from the top of the hill.

Name:

Fearless suffixes

- Underline all the words using **less** or **ful** suffixes.

It seemed like a hopeless ambition. Despite his careful preparation and fearless training, he thought he would never be able to get to the summit. His powerful muscles were straining at the effort he asked of them. Jacob's colourful shirt was visible against the beautiful snowy background.

- Sort the words you have underlined into groups.

less	**ful**

- What is the rule for adding a suffix to a word ending in **y**?

____

____.

- Add **ful** or **less** to these words.

pity → ____________________

plenty → ____________________

Using 'er' and 'est'

Objective

Use the suffixes 'er' and 'est' in adjectives.

Background knowledge

Adjectives can show the degree to which a noun possesses a particular quality. This is done by using three different forms of adjective:

- The main adjective or 'nominative', such as *The tree is tall.*
- The 'comparative' suggests a comparison between a noun or another noun, such as *This tree is taller.*
- The 'superlative' shows that this noun is the extreme example of a particular quality, such as *This tree is tallest.*

These terms do not need to be used with children at Key Stage 1. Instead you can say:
Add 'er' to compare two nouns: *small – smaller.*
Add 'est' when comparing more than two nouns: *small – smallest.*
For adjectives ending in 'y', remind children to change the 'y' to 'i' before adding 'er' or 'est'.

Activities

- **Photocopiable page 48 'Tall, taller, tallest'**
Write the endings 'er' and 'est' on the board. Explain that these endings are added to adjectives so that we can compare objects. Ask two children to stand up. Ask: *Who is taller?* Say: *X is tall, but Y is taller.* Explain that we add 'er' to 'tall' to make 'taller', because we are comparing two children. Now ask another child to stand up. Ask: *Now, who is tallest?* Invite a child to put the three children in height order. Say: *X is tall, Y is taller, but Z is tallest.* Explain that we usually add 'er' to adjectives to compare two objects, but if there are more than two, we add 'est'. Challenge the children to work through the photocopiable sheet adding 'er' and 'est' to words.

- **Photocopiable page 49 'Which order?'**
Show the children three lengths of string. Invite a child to put them in length order, with the shortest first. Ask: *Which is the longest?* Invite a child to write a label and match it to the string. Repeat for 'longer' and 'long'. Explain to the children that they should order sets of adjectives from the least to the most. Then they should choose appropriate adjectives to complete sentences.

- **Photocopiable page 50 'Weather chart'**
This photocopiable sheet is about adding 'er' and 'est' to adjectives ending in 'y'. Write the word 'snowy' on the board. Explain that to add a suffix to it, you need to change the 'y' to an 'i' and then add the suffix. 'Snowy' becomes 'snowier' or 'snowiest'. Show children the weather chart. Ask questions about the chart, such as: *What was the weather like on Tuesday in week 1?* When children are confident interpreting the chart, challenge them to complete the weather report, changing 'y' to 'i', then adding 'er' or 'est'.

Further ideas

- **My grandma's cat:** Play this game with the children. Start off saying: *My grandma's cat was a fluffy cat.* The next child should say: *My grandma's cat was the fluffier cat.* The final child should say: *My grandma's cat was the fluffiest cat.* The next child starts again, choosing a new adjective. Vary the game by substituting 'cat' for another animal or object.

Digital content

On the digital component you will find:

- Printable versions of all three photocopiable pages.
- Answers to all three photocopiable pages.
- Interactive versions of all three photocopiable pages.

Name:

Using 'er' and 'est'

Tall, taller, tallest?

To compare two objects we often add **er**.

To compare more than two objects we often add **est**.

■ Add **er** or **est** to the words below.

Name:

Using 'er' and 'est'

Which order?

■ Order the adjectives, from least to most.

1. strongest strong stronger

2. kinder kindest kind

3. rough roughest rougher

■ Choose an adjective for each sentence.

longer	rougher	sweeter	smoother

1. An apple is ______________ than a pineapple.
2. A mango is ______________ than a lemon.
3. A cucumber is ______________ than a potato.
4. A cauliflower is ______________ than a carrot.

Name:

Using 'er' and 'est'

Weather chart

	Mon	Tues	Wed	Thurs	Fri	Sat	Sun
Week 1							
Week 2							

sunny rainy
cloudy windy

To add **er** or **est**: change **y** to **i**.

- Use the weather chart to finish the report.
- Use **er** and **est** endings.

1. Week 1 was sunny but week 2 was ______________ .
2. Week 1 was cloudy but week 2 was ______________ .
3. Week 2 was rainless, so week 1 was ______________ .
4. Thursdays were the ______________ day.
5. Wednesday of week 1 was the only ______________ day.

- Write your own sentence, using the chart to help you.

____

____

Adverbs

Objective

Recognise and understand the function of adverbs.

Background knowledge

Adverbs tell us about verbs – they describe and give more detail about the verb. They can tell us how something happened (the manner of a verb), where something happened (the place of a verb), or when something happened (the time of a verb). These are adverbs of manner, place and time. Adverbs often end with the suffix 'ly'. Children in Year 2 need to know the term 'adverb' and to understand that they describe the verb. For example, *Scamp ran across the field* only tells us that *Scamp ran*, it does not tell us how she ran. If we say, *Scamp ran quickly across the field*, the adverb 'quickly' describes how she ran.

Activities

- **Photocopiable page 52 'How do they do it?'**
Invite the children to give examples of verbs and list them on the board. Ask: *What is a verb?* Explain that verbs are 'doing words' – they tell us what we do. Explain that adverbs are words that tell us about the verb – they tell us how we did it. Ask: *What are you doing?* List a few suggestions. Choose one and ask about it. For example: *How are you listening?* List suggestions, such as *quietly* and *calmly*. Tell the children that adverbs often end with the suffix 'ly'. Challenge the children to find the adverbs within the sentences and to think of their own adverbs for each verb on the photocopiable sheet. Finish by sharing the adverbs and sentences the children used.
- **Photocopiable page 53 'Making adverbs'**
Explain that adverbs can be made by adding the suffix 'ly' to some adjectives. Write the words 'bad', 'soft' and 'happy' on the board. Invite children to write 'ly' after each one. Make sure that children know they should change the 'y' in 'happy' to an 'i'. Explain that these are now adverbs, so they can be used to tell us about a verb. Challenge children to work in pairs to write a sentence using each of these adverbs. Then ask the children to create adverbs on the photocopiable sheet and to use these in sentences. Finish by asking children to read their sentences. Ask: *What does the adverb tell us in this sentence?*
- **Photocopiable page 54 'Silly sentences (2)'**
Read the words on the photocopiable sheet with the children. Explain that they should make three piles of cards, and use these to make sentences. They should write the sentences down as they make them. Invite the children to read out their sentences to the class. Then challenge them to make sentences that start with the adverb. Ask: *Does it change the meaning of your sentence?* Explain that adverbs can come after verbs, but they do not have to. They still describe the verb, even when they start a sentence.

Further ideas

- **Making choices:** Challenge children to write a sentence that contains an adverb. Then ask them to think of three alternative adverbs that would also make sense. Repeat with other sentences. Children could use these words to create a bank of adverbs, which they could then refer to during independent writing.

Digital content

On the digital component you will find:

- Printable versions of all three photocopiable pages.
- Answers to 'How do they do it?' and 'Making adverbs'.
- Interactive versions of 'How do they do it?' and 'Making adverbs'.

Name:

Adverbs

How do they do it?

■ Underline the **adverbs** in each sentence. The first one has been done for you.

Tip: They usually end with **ly**.

1. The dog ran quickly through the grass.
2. Leon ate his breakfast greedily.
3. Katy gently stroked the cat.
4. Anwar's book fell heavily to the floor.
5. Slowly the moon appeared from behind the cloud.

■ Write an adverb for each verb.

Verb	Adverb
danced	
ate	
swam	
climbed	

■ Choose a verb and an adverb and write your own sentence using them.

____

____.

Making adverbs

■ Change these adjectives into adverbs by adding **ly** to the end.

■ If the word ends with **y**, change it to **i**.

1. weak ________

2. kind ________

3. quiet ________
4. happy ________
5. creepy ________
6. angry ________

+ ly

■ Use some of the adverbs you have made to finish these sentences.

1. The stray dog ________________.
2. The ancient house ________________.
3. The shiny parcel ________________.

Name:

Adverbs

Silly sentences (2)

- In the table below, colour the nouns red, the verbs blue and the adverbs yellow.
- Cut out the cards and put them in three piles.
- Choose a card from each pile to make a sentence.
- Write your sentences on a separate sheet of paper.

Noun	Verb	Adverb
The doctor	sang	carefully
Sam	purred	gently
Tiger	stirred	madly
Everyone	danced	mysteriously
The witch	listened	angrily

Writing with adjectives

Objective

Write effectively for purpose using adjectives.

Background knowledge

Adjectives, as well as making descriptive writing more interesting, can also be used to add a degree of precision to communication. Encourage children to build up a collection of adjectives on a theme, to allow them to experiment with the degrees of meaning. They could find different adjectives that are similar to the adjective *hungry*. Discuss how meaning changes with the different variations. Is *hungry* weaker in meaning than *famished* or *starving*? When would it be appropriate to use each adjective in a sentence? Invite children to explore how adjectives can be changed by using prefixes or suffixes and to use them in their own writing.

Activities

- **Photocopiable page 56 'On the beach'**

Put a selection of objects on a table, making sure there are different numbers of items in various colours, for example: three pencils (one red, two green), two rubbers and a blue cup. Ask the children to describe the objects using colour and number words. Explain to them that they are using describing words. Tell the children that you want them to colour in the picture on the sheet and then write about it. Remind them to use colour and number words as they did during the whole-class work. After writing, encourage children to re-read their work, editing it to make improvements.

- **Photocopiable page 57 'Choc Chews'**

Read through the Choc Chews advert and ask the children what they think of it. Do the sweets sound exciting? Why not? Read out the words at the bottom of the page and then ask the children to use some of them (and some of their own) to make the advert more appealing. Ask one child to read out the original advert, and ask another child to read out their rewritten one. Which one would encourage the children to buy the sweets? Ask the children to write a sentence or two about sweets that they like, again using exciting and persuasive adjectives. After writing, ask children to share their work with a partner to help them edit and improve their writing further.

- **Photocopiable page 58 'Describe someone'**

Introduce this activity by working through a shared version of it first. Display a photograph of a person and ask the children to suggest adjectives to describe them. List their suggestions on the board. Then ask the children to make up some sentences about the person, using adjectives from the list. Now ask the children to cut out a picture from a magazine and to work through the process you have practised together to complete the photocopiable sheet.

Further ideas

- **Improving writing:** Ask children to look back at some of their own completed pieces of writing. Can they see places where they could have used adjectives or adverbs to make the writing more interesting?
- **Story map:** Ask pairs of children to choose one of the people they described on photocopiable page 58 'Describe someone' and make up a story with that person as the main character. They should create a story map, making notes on the beginning, middle and end of their story and jotting down adjectives to describe the other characters and the setting. They should also include adverbs to make their writing more interesting.
- **Persuasive adjectives:** What are the best things about your school? Ask groups of children to write a leaflet to give to children who are starting at the school. They should use persuasive adjectives and adverbs to emphasise the really good things about it and make their writing more interesting.

Digital content

On the digital component you will find:

- Printable versions of all three photocopiable pages.

Name:

Writing with adjectives

On the beach

■ Colour in the picture. Then write about it, using colour and number words.

Name:

Writing with adjectives

Choc Chews

- Rewrite this advert using words that are more exciting than **nice**. Some words are given below to help you.
- Use the back of this sheet to write about your favourite sweets.

Buy these **nice** sweets.

They taste **nice**.

They are **nice**.

Choc Chews make you feel **nice**.

Get some now!

Buy these ______________________ sweets.

They taste ______________________ .

They are ______________________ .

Choc Chews make you feel ______________ .

Get some now!

fantastic amazing enormous giant
brilliant wicked great sad
wonderful delicious scrummy yummy

Name:

Writing with adjectives

Describe someone

■ Stick a photograph of someone here. List words that describe him or her.

■ Write two sentences about your person, using some of the describing words from your list.

Chapter 3

Verbs

Introduction

The aim of this chapter is to enable children to discover the function and explore the variety of verbs. Children need to be able to use both the present and past tense accurately in their own writing and are given opportunities to explore the way verbs change to show tense. They are encouraged to use their creativity to develop their use of verbs in real and imaginary settings. They are invited to describe themselves and to search for verbs to use in stories and persuasive writing. Many early years classes begin by using the term 'doing word' but will need to move on to using the term 'verb' in Year 2. For further practice, please see the 'Verbs' section of the Years 1–2 workbook.

Poster notes

Verbs (page 60)

This poster presents a variety of verbs that can be used instead of 'go' and 'say'. Explore the differences in meaning with the children. How is 'dash' different from 'crawl'? Act out some of the verbs. Ask the children questions to encourage them to explore the other verbs. Encourage them to refer to the poster when they are writing stories.

Verb tenses (page 61)

This poster offers examples of the ways in which words change when the tense changes. Display it in the classroom. Cover the bold verb in one column and ask the children to supply the missing verb in the appropriate tense. Ask children to suggest other past tense verbs that end in 'ed'.

In this chapter

Vocabulary

In Year 1 children need to know:
doing word, singular, plural, sentence, now, past

In Year 2 children need to know:
verb, tense, past tense, present tense, suffix

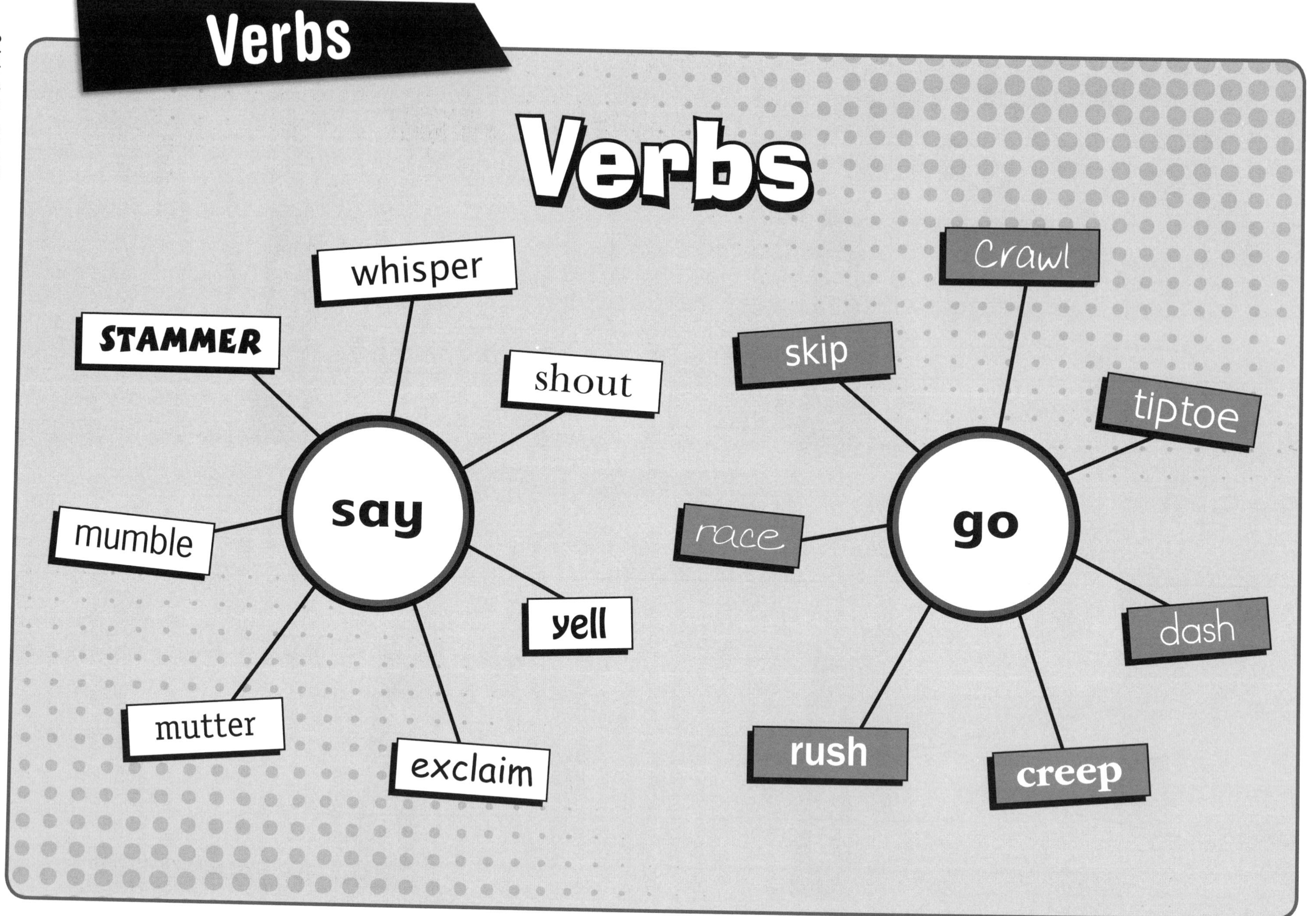
Verbs
Verbs
say
whisper
STAMMER
shout
mumble
yell
mutter
exclaim
go
Crawl
skip
tiptoe
race
dash
rush
creep

Verbs

Verb tenses

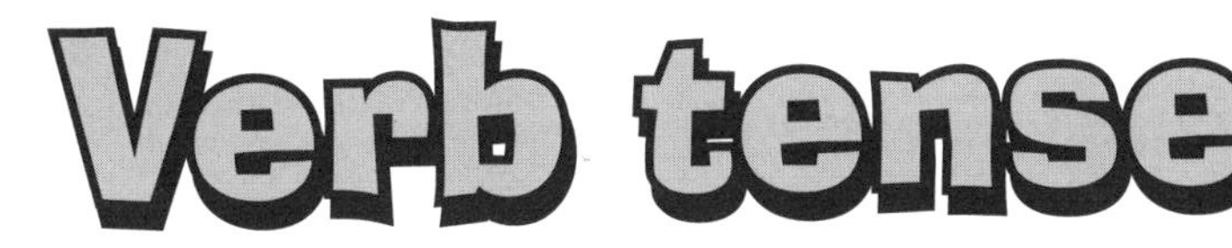

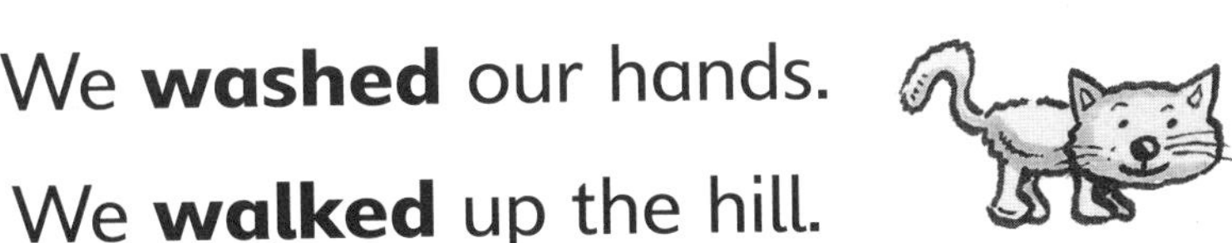

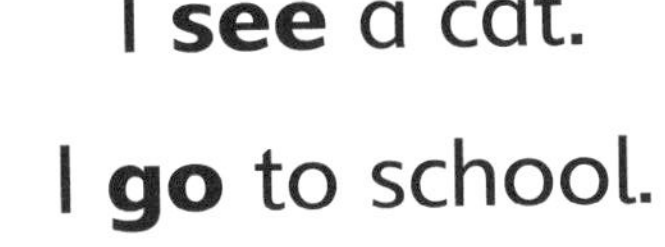

Today	Yesterday
I **help** my mum.	I **helped** my mum.
We **wash** our hands.	We **washed** our hands.
We **walk** up the hill.	We **walked** up the hill.
We **look** at the hats.	We **looked** at the hats.
I **see** a cat.	I **saw** a cat.
I **go** to school.	I **went** to school.
We **say**, "Hello."	We **said**, "Hello."

What is a verb?

Objective

Recognise and understand the function of verbs in sentences.

Background knowledge

A verb is a word that tells us what action or state is taking place. In the sentence *I ate the cake*, the verb is 'ate'. Verbs are sometimes referred to as 'doing words'. Children do not need to be introduced to the term 'verb' until Year 2. Remind children about the groups of words they know about: naming words/ nouns; describing words/adjectives. Tell them they are going to look at a group of words that tell us what is happening in a sentence, for example 'sitting', 'reading' or 'swimming'. Together, think of as many as you can. Explain that inserting the prefix 'un' changes the meaning of verbs to their opposite, so *tie* becomes *untie*.

Activities

- **Photocopiable page 63 'What can you do?'**
Tell the children some of the things you can do – *walk*, *skate*, *drive*, *play the piano* and so on. Then ask them to tell you some of the things they can do. Ask them to write four of the things they can do on the photocopiable sheet. Explain that they can use the words given or think of their own. They should then finish the sentences about birds and dogs. Finally, ask them to think of another group of creatures (real or imaginary) and say what those creatures can do. (For example, *Fish can…* or *Dragons can…*)
- **Photocopiable page 64 'My monster'**
You can prepare for this activity by sharing a large illustration of an imaginary character (possibly from a story the children have read). Ask the children to imagine what the character might do if he were angry – for example, he might shout or bellow. What about if he was sad? Ask them to create their own monster and write about it, using the sentence starters on the sheet.
- **Photocopiable page 65 'Opposites'**
Write the prefix 'un' on the board. Explain that this prefix can be used to changed the meaning of a verb. Write the word 'cover' on the board. Invite the children to read the word and to use it in a sentence. Now invite a child to write the prefix 'un' before it. Ask: *What does the word say now? How has the meaning changed?* Can the children think of other verbs that can be changed in this way? Use the photocopiable sheet to write new verbs using 'un' and to create some sentences.

Further ideas

- **Homework:** Ask the children to list verbs that describe what they do after school and through the evening – *eating*, *playing*, *washing* and so on.
- **Shared reading:** During shared reading using a Big Book, ask the children to tell you which is the verb in each sentence as you read. Can they suggest some alternatives that would fit in the sentence? Then ask the children to take a piece of their own writing and underline the verbs, thinking of others that they could have used instead.
- **Finding verbs:** When you are writing lists of tasks the children are going to be working on, ask the children to point out the verb each time – for example *finish*, *write* or *copy*.

Digital content

On the digital component you will find:

- Printable versions of all three photocopiable pages.
- Answers to 'Opposites'.
- Interactive version of 'Opposites'.

Name:

What is a verb?

What can you do?

■ Use the words in the box, or your own words, to finish these sentences.

I can ____ .

I can ____ .

I can ____ .

I can ____ .

Birds can ____ .

Dogs can ____ .

■ Think of another type of animal. What can it do?

______________________ can ______________________ .

read	fly	run	hop
bark	eat	jump	sleep

Name:

What is a verb?

My monster

■ Draw a monster. Finish the sentences by saying what he likes to do.

When my monster is cross he likes to

____ .

When he is happy he likes to ______________________ .

When he is sad he likes to ________________________ .

In school, he likes to ____________________________ .

At home, he likes to _____________________________ .

In the park, he likes to ___________________________ .

Best of all, he likes to ___________________________ .

What is a verb?

Opposites

■ Add **un** to each verb below.

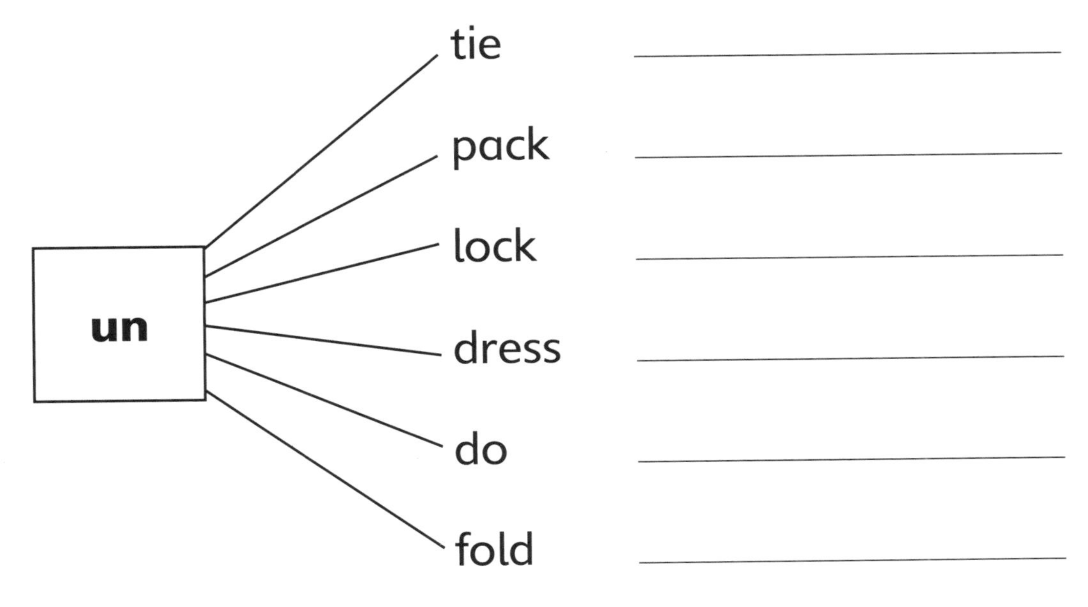

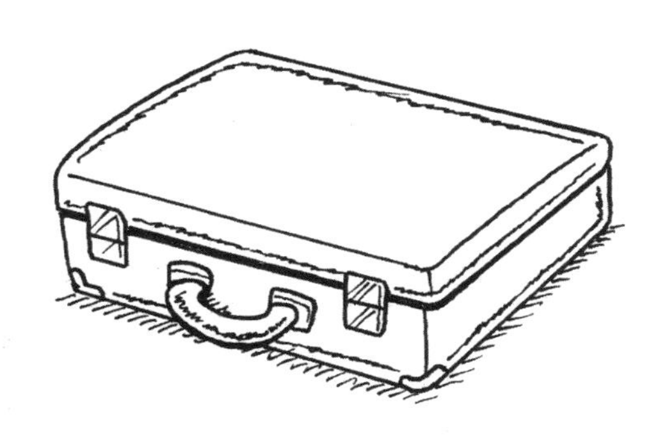

■ Use these words in sentences.

pack **unpack**

____

____

____

____

Verbs – present and past tense (1)

Objective

Use the present and past tenses correctly.

Background knowledge

It is necessary to make explicit the knowledge children already have of things happening in the past and present. Ask children what they are doing now, encouraging them to answer in sentences (for example: *I am looking at the book*). Explain that these things are happening in the present or now. Ask them to tell you what they did yesterday (*I looked*) and explain that this is something that happened in the past, so we use the past tense. Verbs change to show when something is happening. Tenses place an action in time. Children in Year 2 should be introduced to the terms 'tense', 'past tense' and 'present tense'.

In English there are two simple tenses:

- **Present tense:** the action is occurring now (*I walk*).
- **Past tense:** the action occurred previously. The common ending for past tense verbs is 'ed' (*I walked*).

For these two tenses the verb stem itself can alter.

Activities

- **Photocopiable page 67 'About me'**

Invite the children to say a sentence describing themselves, such as: *I have red hair*. Write a few examples on the board. Explain these are all about things that are happening now so they use 'doing words' that show it is now. Invite the children to complete the sentences on the photocopiable sheet, choosing the correct 'doing word'. Ask the children to answer the questions using sentences. Explain that the 'doing words' they have used all show that it is happening now.

- **Photocopiable page 68 'Yesterday'**

Write a few sentences in the present tense, such as: *I am listening to music. My brother watches television.* Tell the children that you did the same thing yesterday and ask them to help you change the sentences into the past tense. Explain that many verbs change to the past tense by adding the 'ed' ending. Ask the children to imagine that everything on the sheet happened yesterday, and to change the sentences from the present to the past tense. Encourage the children to re-read their writing. In shared writing, demonstrate how to edit or make corrections.

- **Photocopiable page 69 'All change!'**

Explain that verbs change to show which tense is being discussed. Write *I play* on the board. Ask: *Which tense is this? How could I change the tense?* Repeat for irregular words, such as *I am*. Ask the children to change the verbs to show present or past tense. Challenge them to rewrite the sentences, changing verbs to the past tense.

Further ideas

- **Charades:** Play a game of charades, asking a child to mime a verb while the other children try to guess what it is.
- **Verb pairs:** Write these verbs on the board: *watched, shout, stop, bit, see, wrote, find, ran, play, won, type, walked, helped, swam, stopped, run, made, win, ate, walk, shouted, help, write, saw, bite, found, eat, typed, draw, played, swim, drew, make, watch.* Ask the children to work in pairs to find the matching pairs of verbs and sort them into present tense and past tense. Challenge them to make up some pairs of their own.

Digital content

On the digital component you will find:

- Printable versions of all three photocopiable pages.
- Answers to all three photocopiable pages.
- Interactive versions of 'About me' and 'All change!'.

About me

■ Choose the correct word.

eat	wear	watch	live	go	have	am

1. Now I ______________ six years old.
2. I ______________ brown hair.
3. I ______________ bananas.
4. I ______________ a jumper.
5. I ______________ to school.
6. I ______________ in a house.
7. I ______________ television.

■ Answer these questions.

8. What is your name?

____

9. What food do you like?

____

10. What day do you do art at school?

____

Name:

Verbs – present and past tense (1)

Yesterday

■ Rewrite these sentences so the events happened in the past. Add **ed** to the doing word.

1. **I walk to school.**

Yesterday, ______________________________ .

2. **They laugh at the clown.**

Yesterday, ______________________________ .

3. **Sammy picks strawberries.**

Yesterday, ______________________________ .

4. **They help the teacher.**

Yesterday, ______________________________ .

5. **We talk to the teacher.**

Yesterday, ______________________________ .

6. **I look at my hands.**

Yesterday, ______________________________ .

■ What did you do yesterday?

____

____

All change!

■ Change these verbs from the present tense to the past tense.

Present tense	Past tense
live	
am	
work	
go	
eat	

■ Change these verbs from the past tense to the present tense.

Past tense	Present tense
looked	
slept	
swam	
were	
sat	

■ Rewrite these sentences in the present tense.

1. The dog licked himself clean.

___

2. Omar sat down quietly.

___

3. Dad played football.

___

Verbs – present and past tense (2)

Objective

Use the present and past tenses correctly and consistently.

Background knowledge

The present tense is used to show events that are happening now. It is also used to show events that are applicable now, such as: *My hair is brown*. The past tense is used to show events that have already happened, which are in the past. Most verbs change to show different tenses. Many verbs add 'ed' to form the past tense. Other verbs are irregular, such as *I am/I was*, but children will need to be able to use them accurately.

Activities

- **Photocopiable page 71 'In the past'**

Write *I go to school* on the board. Ask: *What tense is this written in?* Invite children to rewrite the sentence in the past tense. Explain that some verbs are irregular and change to the past tense in different ways. Ask the children to change the sentences on the sheet from the present to the past tense, imagining that everything happened yesterday. Encourage the children to re-read their writing, checking for consistent use of tenses.

- **Photocopiable page 72 'When I was little'**

Ask the children to tell you about some of the things that they did when they were little. Encourage them to answer in sentences in the simple past tense, such as *I crawled*. Ask them if they still do those things and, if not, what they do instead, for example *I walk* or *I run*. Read through the photocopiable sheet, explaining to the children that they should write about themselves as they are now, and compare each situation to what they would have done when they were little.

- **Photocopiable page 73 'Jack and the Beanstalk'**

Remind the children that stories are usually told in the past tense – as if things happened a long time ago. Together, briefly retell the story of 'Jack and the Beanstalk', then explain that the beginning of that story is on the photocopiable sheet. All the 'doing words' (verbs) are in the present tense, and the children need to write the past tense forms in the gaps. When they have finished, ask them to think about what happened next and to write the rest of the story, continuing in the past tense.

Further ideas

- **Shared reading:** During shared reading of a story, point out to the children that the story is told as if the events have already happened. Read a section of your chosen text, changing the verbs into the present tense, and ask the children to tell you how this changes the story.
- **Consistency:** When children are writing their own stories, remind them to use the past tense. Encourage them to re-read their writing, checking they have been consistent in their use of tenses.

Digital content

On the digital component you will find:

- Printable versions of all three photocopiable pages.
- Answers to 'In the past' and 'Jack and the Beanstalk'.
- Interactive version of 'Jack and the Beanstalk'.

Verbs – present and past tense (2)

In the past

■ Rewrite these sentences so the events happened in the past.

1. **They go shopping.**

Yesterday, ______________________________.

2. **I have a bath.**

Last night, ______________________________.

3. **Mum takes the dog for a walk.**

Yesterday, ______________________________.

4. **We swim in the big pool.**

Last Saturday, ______________________________.

5. **I sing a new song.**

Last week, ______________________________.

■ What did you see on your way to school?

____

____

■ What did you eat last night?

____

____

Name:

Verbs – present and past tense (2)

When I was little

■ Write about yourself now. Then write similar sentences about yourself in the past.

Now I am ______________________________ .

When I was little I ______________________________ .

Now I like ______________________________ .

When I was little I ______________________________ .

Now I eat ______________________________ .

When I was little I ______________________________ .

Now I wear ______________________________ .

When I was little I ______________________________ .

Now I ______________________________ .

When I was little I ______________________________ .

Verbs – present and past tense (2)

Jack and the Beanstalk

- Write the story as if it happened a long time ago, changing the verbs to fit the gaps.
- Write what you think happens next on another sheet of paper.

Jack and his mother ____________ poor, but
(are)

they ____________ a cow. Jack ____________
(have) (goes)

to market and he ____________ it.
(sells)

Then he ____________ home.
(walks)

He ____________ his mother
(shows)

what he ____________ for the cow.
(gets)

"Beans!" she ____________ . "That's no
(shouts)

good!" She ____________ so angry that she
(is)

____________ the beans out of the window.
(throws)

Next morning...

Verbs – action in progress

Objective

Use the progressive form of verbs in the present and past tense to mark actions in progress.

Background knowledge

The present tense can be formed by combining the main verb with an auxiliary verb or 'helper verb', such as: *I like baking*. The present progressive tense is used to show continuing action, something going on now. This tense is formed with the present tense of the verb 'to be', plus the present tense of the main verb with an 'ing' ending: *I am looking at a book; They are walking the dog.*

The past progressive tense shows continuous action in the past. It is formed with the past tense of the verb 'to be', plus the present tense of the main verb with an 'ing' ending: *I was looking at a book; They were walking the dog.* Children do not need to know the terms present progressive or past progressive verbs at this stage. They do need to be able to use them.

Activities

- **Photocopiable page 75 'What I like doing'**

Sometimes the present tense can be made with a 'helper verb' and the main verb. The main verb ends in 'ing'. In this activity the 'helper verb' is *like*. Ask the children to list verbs to state what they like doing and what they don't like doing. There are suggested verbs given, but you may like to come up with others together.

- **Photocopiable page 76 'Helper verbs'**

Explain that there are 'being verbs' and 'doing verbs'. The being verbs are: *am, is, are, was, were*. These can be put with doing verbs, such as *playing*, to form more present or past tense verbs that describe an action which is continually or has been continually occurring. Ask the children to work in pairs to play the game. Children should say their sentences to their partner and then write it down. They need to sort their sentences into present and past tense.

- **Photocopiable page 77 'Busy pets'**

Explain that the children should use the 'being' verbs to change the sentences. Tell them that they will also need to change the doing word to make it 'agree' with the 'being' verb. As an example, use the verb 'watch' and change it to 'am watching'. Ask: *How did the word 'watch' change? How has the meaning of the sentence changed? Is this past or present tense?*

Further ideas

- **Homework:** Ask the children to list verbs that describe what they do after school and through the evening – *eating, playing, washing* and so on.
- **Storytime:** During shared reading, ask children to find verbs that are made using a 'helper verb'. Make a list and ask children to suggest new sentences using these verbs.
- **Now and then:** Challenge children to say an action in the present tense (such as *I am swimming*) and then to change it into the past tense (*I was swimming*). Ask: *Which words are the verbs?*

Digital content

On the digital component you will find:

- Printable versions of all three photocopiable pages.
- Answers to 'Busy pets'.

Verbs – action in progress

What I like doing

■ Write lists of things you like doing and things you don't like doing. You can use some of the words below.

I like | **I don't like**

helping	camping	jumping
talking	singing	washing
cooking	laughing	walking
tidying	reading	playing

I am good at ______________________.

I want to get better at ______________________.

Name:

Verbs – action in progress

Helper verbs

- Cut out the word cards below.
- Make two piles: **Being verbs** and **Doing verbs**.
- Take a word card from each pile.
- Use these words in a sentence and write it on a separate sheet of paper.
- Was your sentence in the present tense or the past tense?
- Can you think of more **Doing verbs** to put with these **Being verbs**? List them on your separate sheet of paper.

Being verbs	**Doing verbs**
am	reading
is	writing
are	drawing
was	running
were	sitting

Busy pets

■ Use one of the being verbs below to change these sentences.

am is are

1. The dog barks.

____.

2. I sleep in bed.

____.

3. The birds sing.

____.

■ Now try these using one of the being verbs below.

was were

4. I stroked the cat.

____.

5. The rabbits hopped in the field.

____.

6. The mouse ate the cheese.

____.

Verbs in writing

Objective

Use verb tenses correctly and consistently in writing.

Background knowledge

Children should be able to explore different types of writing and appreciate the ways in which verbs are used differently according to text type. The following activities offer opportunities to explore more adventurous verbs, write a set of instructions and a story.

Activities

- **Photocopiable page 79 'Little Red Riding Hood'**
Read out the story of 'Little Red Riding Hood' from the photocopiable sheet, inserting the word 'said' in each of the gaps. Help the children to appreciate that the story could be much more interesting if the author had sometimes used words other than 'said'. Tell the children to rewrite the story, filling all the gaps with interesting verbs. There is a selection given at the bottom of the page, but the children may be able to suggest their own. Afterwards, compare different versions and talk about the effects.
- **Photocopiable page 80 'Instructions for an alien'**
Ask each child to instruct another child to perform a simple task. (*Stand up. Put your hands on your head.*) Ask children to name the verb in each of these instructions. Ask them to complete the photocopiable sheet with instructions for an alien. As well as using a variety of verbs, this activity looks at words used to link events in time (*first*, *next*, *then* and so on). These words tend to begin sentences and serve to link a sentence to what has gone before.
- **Photocopiable page 81 'The journey'**
Invite different children to read out the top verb from each list and then to read the alternative verbs. Challenge them to think of sentences using some of the new verbs. Can they think of other verbs? Read the passage with the children. Discuss how changing the verbs could make the passage more interesting. Ask the children to write about their own imaginary journey, using some of the better verbs suggested. Encourage them to think of their own interesting verbs. Invite children to read out their journeys and ask other children to discuss the effectiveness of the verbs used. When they have finished, ask them to re-read their work, checking that the tenses have been used correctly and consistently, correcting any errors.

Further ideas

- **Poems:** Write out familiar poems, omitting occasional verbs. Invite the children to write their own versions of the poem by filling the spaces with their own verbs. Remind them that it does not matter which verb they choose as long as it agrees with the other words.
- **Better verbs:** In pairs, the children can look through books for words that have been used instead of 'said' and 'went'. These can be listed and shared with the class. Ask children to look through some of their own writing and see if there are places where some of these words could have been used. Tell them to replace a few and read the old and then the new sentence out loud. What effect does the new word have?
- **Move on!:** During PE ask children to suggest verbs for the way they are moving, such as *creeping*, *crawling*, *jumping*, *jogging*, *bouncing* and so on. Collect these together in a picture glossary, with a picture to match each verb. Encourage the children to use these in their writing.

Digital content

On the digital component you will find:

- Printable versions of all three photocopiable pages.

Verbs in writing

Little Red Riding Hood

■ Fill in the gaps in this story by using more interesting words than **said**. There are some words at the bottom of the page to help you.

"Hello, little girl," ____growled____ the wolf.

Little Red Riding Hood felt scared. "Hello, Mr Wolf," she ______________.

"Where are you going?" ______________ the wolf.

"To visit my grandma," ______________ Little Red Riding Hood.

"Can I come with you?" the wolf ______________.

"No!" ______________ Little Red Riding Hood, and she ran away as fast as she could.

shouted called whispered growled
asked answered yelled hissed muttered

Name:

Verbs in writing

Instructions for an alien

■ Complete the instructions below to help an alien to get ready in the morning. Use these phrases:

have breakfast get out of bed get dressed

First ______________________________.

Next ______________________________.

Then ______________________________.

■ Use words and pictures to tell the alien what to do when he gets to school. Draw the last picture.

First ______________________________.

Next ______________________________.

Then ______________________________.

Verbs in writing

The journey

■ Read this text about a journey.

I looked at the aeroplane. It was going soon. I had to run to the check-in desk. I was cross because my sister was walking slowly. I didn't make a fuss.

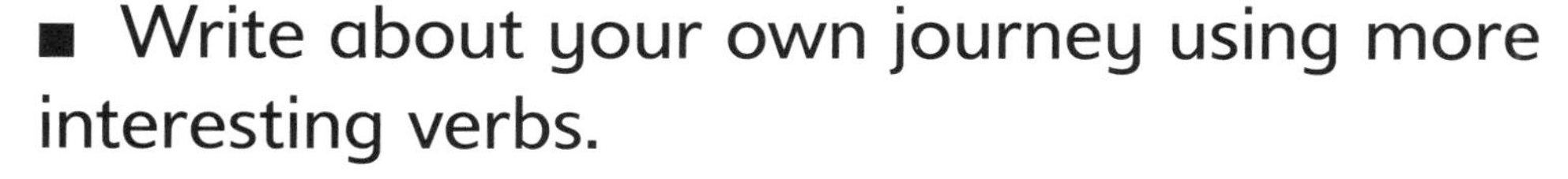

■ Write about your own journey using more interesting verbs.

looked	**go**	**run**	**walk**	**make**
glared	depart	jog	saunter	create
watched	move	sprint	amble	build
gazed	leave	dash	stroll	construct
stared	disappear	hurry	wander	assemble
searched		gallop		

Chapter 4

Sentences (1)

Introduction

This chapter focuses on identifying and writing sentences. The sections look at the use of a capital letter to mark the beginning of a sentence and at the use of punctuation to mark the end of a sentence. There is also an emphasis on understanding that a sentence must make sense and that it is not the same as a line of text. For further practice, please see the 'Sentences (1)' section of the Years 1–2 workbook.

Poster notes

What is a sentence? (page 83)
Some children find it quite hard to differentiate a group of words or a line of writing from a sentence. This poster offers three criteria for identifying a sentence. It can be enlarged and displayed as a reminder to the children when they are engaged in their own writing. They can use it as a checklist when they re-read what they have written.

Check your writing (page 84)
Children can be encouraged to re-read their writing, bearing in mind the points on this checklist. It can be enlarged and displayed as a permanent reminder. You may suggest that children read their work aloud in a quiet voice to notice where they would naturally pause and to check that their punctuation reflects this.

In this chapter

Vocabulary

In Year 1 children need to know:
letter, capital letter, sentence, punctuation, full stop, question mark, joining word

In Year 2 children need to know:
statement, question, command, joining word

Sentences (1)

What is a sentence

A sentence begins with a capital letter.

He has a new bike.

A sentence ends with . ? or !

My name is Liz.

What is your name?

Watch out!

Watch Out!

A sentence makes sense.

long tail ✗

My dog has a long tail. ✓

Sentences (1)

Check your writing

Have I started every sentence with a capital letter? ✓

Have I used full stops where they are needed? ✓

Have I ended every question with a question mark? ✓

Have I used exclamation marks correctly? ✓

What is a sentence?

Objective

Recognise and identify the features of a sentence.

Background knowledge

A sentence is a unit of language that makes sense on its own. It can be a statement, a question, a command or an exclamation. In writing, a sentence begins with a capital letter and ends with a full stop, question mark or exclamation mark. These activities focus on punctuation. A capital letter is not a punctuation mark but its function in starting a sentence is taught at the same time as the full stop.

Children develop a growing awareness of sentences through their reading and writing. They often write sentences but leave out the punctuation marks. Reading aloud, taking account of punctuation that indicates pauses and changes of intonation, will help to demonstrate the purposes of punctuation.

Activities

- **Photocopiable page 86 'Capital letters and full stops'**

Read through the poem with the children. Explain to them that the poem has been written incorrectly – there are no capital letters or full stops. Write a similar 'wrong' sentence on the board (for example: *my cat is ill*). Tell them to correct the sentences on the sheet by sticking the capital letters over the appropriate lower-case letters and then adding full stops.

- **Photocopiable page 87 'Grandma'**

Remind the children that sentences begin with a capital letter and usually end with a full stop. Also explain that a sentence is not the same as a line of writing – a sentence makes sense by itself. Ask them to read what the characters on the sheet say and circle the capital letters and full stops. They should then count how many sentences there are in each speech bubble and write the number on the line. Finally, encourage them to imagine what Grandma is saying at the bottom of the page and write sentences of their own.

- **Photocopiable page 88 'Leela'**

Read through the story extracts about Leela. Ask the children to tell you where they think you should pause as you re-read each paragraph. Remind them that a sentence must make sense on its own. Let the children predict what happens next and write two or three sentences about it. More confident children can work in pairs with their own copy of the activity. They should read through each passage aloud, then note the number of sentences. Talk about any different answers together.

Further ideas

- **Shared reading:** In shared reading, focus on the beginnings and endings of sentences. Ask children to find the capital letters that begin sentences and the punctuation that ends them.
- **Shared writing:** To emphasise that a sentence is not the same as a line of writing, write a verse from the poster 'What is a sentence?' on page 83, changing the line breaks. Show the children that the number of sentences has remained the same. As you are working through some shared writing, write each sentence with a different-coloured pen.
- **Completing sentences:** On a page of a Big Book, find a line of text that comprises one complete sentence plus the beginning of another. Cover up the rest of the text then read the line. Ask the children: *Is it a sentence? Where does the sentence end?* Someone could show you the full stop that ends one sentence and the capital letter that begins the next. Now focus on the second, unfinished sentence. Ask: *Does it make sense?* Can the children suggest ways of completing it? See if they can prompt you to add the appropriate punctuation mark at the end.

Digital content

On the digital component you will find:

- Printable versions of all three photocopiable pages.
- Answers to all three photocopiable pages.
- Interactive version of 'Capital letters and full stops'.

Name:

What is a sentence?

Capital letters and full stops

■ Cut out the capital letters and stick them in the right places. Add the full stops.

this boy had a dog

that boy had a rat

my nan had a kangaroo

what do you think of that?

this girl had a fish

that girl had a cat

my nan had an elephant

what do you think of that?

M

What is a sentence?

Grandma

■ Put circles around the capital letters and full stops in each bubble.

Put on your coat. Then we can go.

I am hungry. I want something to eat.

There are _____ sentences. There are _____ sentences.

I want my mum. She is at home. I want to go home.

Come with me, Grandma. Come and play. We can play football.

There are _____ sentences. There are _____ sentences.

What is Grandma saying?

____

____

____

Name:

What is a sentence?

Leela

■ Write in the capital letters and full stops, then count the sentences.

it was cold Leela wanted

to go out her mother

gave her a hat she put

it on

There are ______ sentences.

Leela went out she saw three

balloons she wanted one Leela

ran after them her mum ran after her

There are ______ sentences.

■ What do you think happened next?

____

____

____

____

Making sense

Objective

Understand that a sentence should make sense and stand alone.

Background knowledge

A 'phrase' is a group of words that are related, expanding on a single word. They do not necessarily make sense on their own. So, for example *the big black dog* is a phrase but not a sentence. A sentence is a group of words that are grammatically connected to each other but not to any words outside the sentence. Ensure children know the word 'sentence' but there is no need to introduce the word 'phrase'. Remind them that a sentence must make sense on its own. Write an incomplete sentence on the board (for example, *I saw a*). Ask the children: *Is this a sentence? Does it begin with a capital letter and end with a punctuation mark?* (It doesn't have both, so it isn't a sentence.) Ask: *If we add a full stop, does it become a sentence?* Explain to the children that this group of words isn't a sentence because it doesn't make sense on its own – there is something missing. Invite them to think of ways of making the words into a sentence, for example: *I saw a dinosaur.*

Activities

- **Photocopiable page 90 'Sentence check'**

Briefly remind the children of what they already know about sentences. The children can work in pairs, reading each group of words and deciding whether or not it is a sentence, and counting how many sentences there are. More confident children can complete those that do not make sense by adding more words and end punctuation.

- **Photocopiable page 91 'Make it fit'**

This activity will develop the children's grammatical skills, helping their awareness of how words combine to make sentences. The sentences on this sheet will be familiar in their sentence structure and vocabulary. The children need to select the right word from a wider choice of words. Encourage the children to try out each word that they think might fit to see if it sounds right in the sentence.

- **Photocopiable page 92 'We like ice cream'**

You may wish to enlarge this sheet for use as a class activity. Read through each group of words and ask the children if each one makes sense. If it doesn't, ask what needs to be added to make it into a sentence. Invite a child to write the full stop in the right place. Then ask the children to look again at the other phrases. What words could they add to make them make sense? The activity could be given to pairs of children to decide which groups of words just need a full stop.

Further ideas

- **Paired work:** Invite the children to write a sentence about themselves and share it with a partner. Together, they can check their writing to see if each has written a proper sentence.
- **Making sentences:** Give the children a selection of words, for example 'I', 'dog', 'a', 'saw', 'cat', 'big' and 'little'. Ask them to work in pairs, making as many different sentences as they can using these words. Remind them that every sentence must begin with a capital letter and end with a full stop or other appropriate punctuation.

Digital content

On the digital component you will find:

- Printable versions of all three photocopiable pages.
- Answers to 'Sentence check' and 'Make it fit'.
- Interactive versions of 'Sentence check' and 'Make it fit'.

Name:

Making sense

Sentence check

■ Which of these are sentences? Use a tick for Yes and a cross for No.

Yes

No

1. This is a big house. ☐
2. Mum is ☐
3. They went to the shop. ☐
4. Look at the ☐
5. That boy is going to school. ☐
6. I want a cake. ☐
7. My cat had kittens. ☐
8. We went out. ☐

■ How many sentences are there? ____________________

Making sense

Make it fit

■ Which of the words from the bottom of the page fits the sentence? Write it in the gap.

1. I ____________ cold.

2. Look at ____________ hat.

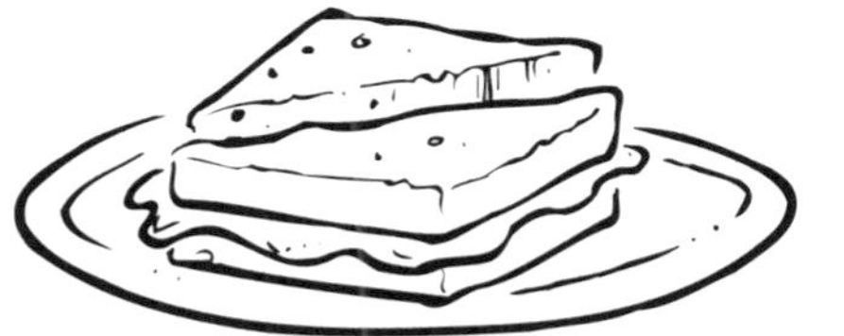

3. I ____________ a sandwich.

4. Put ____________ this hat.

5. Do ____________ want an apple?

6. ____________ you like dogs?

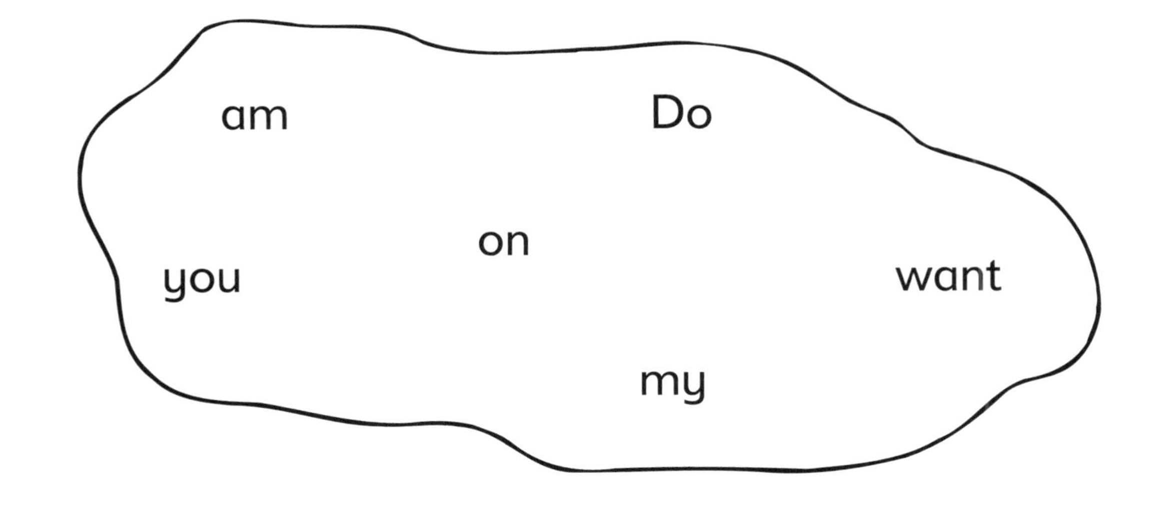

Name:

Making sense

We like ice cream

■ Add words and full stops to make these sentences make sense.

1. It is a ________________

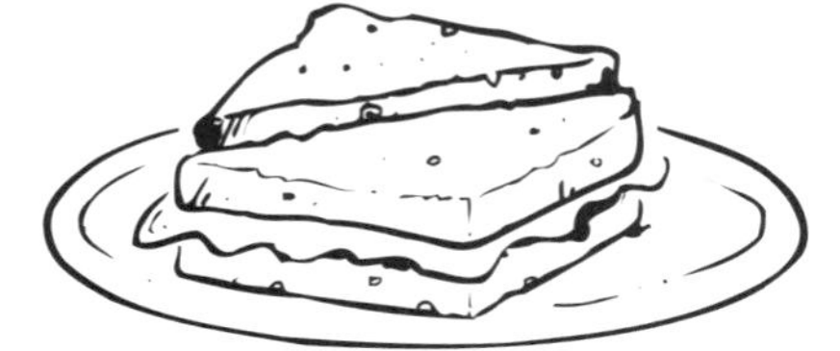

2. I am cold ________________

3. I want a ________________

4. I want something to eat ________________

5. It is a red car ________________

6. Look at the ________________

7. We like ice cream ________________

8. Put on your ________________

9. We can go to ________________

10. I like school ________________

Using 'and' or 'but'

Objective

Join words and join clauses using 'and' or 'but'.

Background knowledge

A conjunction links two words or phrases together. There are two main types of conjunction:

- coordinating conjunctions (such as *and*) link two words or phrases together as an equal pair
- subordinating conjunctions (such as *when*) introduce a subordinate clause.

Conjunctions have sometimes been referred to as 'connectives'. At this stage children are introduced to the coordinating conjunctions of 'and' and 'but'. They are not introduced to the term 'conjunction' until Year 3. You may wish to use the term 'joining word'.

Activities

- **Photocopiable page 94 'And'**

Explain that short sentences or phrases can be joined using the word 'and'. The word 'and' tells us there is more information. Write *Here is a cat. The cat is furry.* on the board. Explain that these would sound better if they were joined together. Ensure that the children know only one capital letter and full stop are needed. Encourage them to use 'it' to replace 'the cat' in the second sentence. Ask the children to cut out the cards on the photocopiable sheet and spread them out. They should choose a start and find an ending that makes sense. They then need to join these sentences or phrases using the word 'and'. They should read the sentences to a partner and finish by writing out one of the sentences.

- **Photocopiable page 95 'But'**

Explain that 'but' is also a word that can be used to join phrases or short sentences. The word 'but' tells us that contrasting information is in the second part of the sentence. Write: *The cat is very friendly. The cat sometimes scratches.* Invite a child to read the sentences. Ask: *What different information is in the second sentence?* Explain that the word 'but' is used to join sentences when the second sentence describes something different or contrasting. Encourage the children to join the sentences on the photocopiable sheet using 'but'. Ensure that children understand that only one capital letter, at the beginning of the sentence, and one full stop, at the end of the sentence, is needed. Ask the children to join the sentences and to make up their own endings for the sentence starters.

- **Photocopiable page 96 'And or but?'**

The children begin by completing sentences that are missing suitable joining words or conjunctions – either 'and' or 'but'. Explain that as well as using 'and' to join two phrases, you can also use the word 'but'. The first two pairs of sentences have the same opening phrases, but the different endings will indicate to the children whether 'and' or 'but' are required. Ask: *Why would we need to use 'but' to join these sentences? What effect does it have on the meaning?* Advise the children to try out both words each time and see which sounds right in context. Remind them of the occasions when each of these conjunctions are used, and then encourage them to think of sentences that could be added to the last two sentence starters on the sheet.

Further ideas

- **Starters:** Give children a sentence starter, such as: *The monster walked through the dark gloomy wood...* or *The children played happily on the sandy beach....* Ask them to use 'and' or 'but' to join this to their own sentence ending.
- **Big Book:** While sharing a Big Book with the children, ask them to find 'and' or 'but' in the sentences. Discuss how these words are used. Can they spot which two sentences are being joined? Are they only used to join sentences?

Digital content

On the digital component you will find:

- Printable versions of all three photocopiable pages.
- Answers to all three photocopiable pages.
- Interactive version of 'And or but?'.

Name:

Using 'and' or 'but'

And

- Cut out the sentences or phrases.
- Choose a sentence beginning.
- Find an ending that makes sense.
- Use **and** to join them.
- Read the new sentence.
- Write one of your sentences on a separate sheet of paper.

and	**and**	**and**	**and**	**and**	**and**

Beginning	**Ending**
I went to the shop	play on the swings.
The dog wagged its tail	we can go outside.
We can go to the park	bought a cake.
The crocodile came out of the water	it was very cold.
We went swimming	said hello to us.
Put on your coat	he looked scary.

But

- Use **but** to join these sentences.

Remember:

- You only need one capital letter and one full stop.
- Get rid of any repetition.

1. We wanted to walk to school. It was raining.

___

2. I like strawberries. I don't like apples.

___

3. We went camping. The field was very muddy.

___

4. The party was entertaining. The clown was scary.

___

- Finish these sentences.

1. The house was very creepy but

___.

2. There's no such thing as monsters but

___.

3. We enjoyed our holiday but

___.

Name:

Using 'and' or 'but'

And or but?

■ Complete these sentences by using **and** or **but**.

1. I went to the park ________ I played football.
2. I went to the park ________ it rained.
3. It was my birthday ________ I didn't have a party.
4. It was my birthday ________ I got lots of cards.

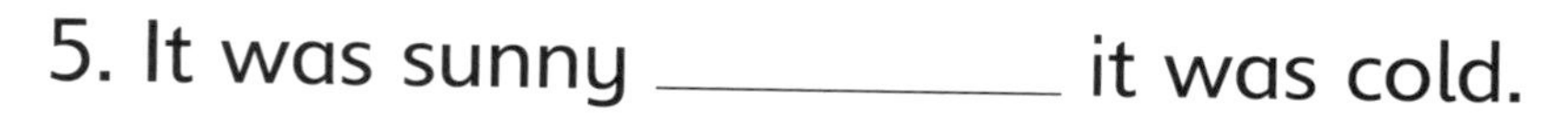

5. It was sunny ________ it was cold.
6. I wanted an ice cream ________ Dad got me one.
7. I got new shoes ________ they didn't fit.

■ Now finish these sentences in your own words.

I went to the park but ________________________________

____.

I went to school and ________________________________

____.

Asking questions

Objective

Identify and compose questions.

Background knowledge

The children should understand what a question is, how it is shown in written text and how it sounds in spoken text. Ask several children a question, such as *How old are you?* or *Do you like chocolate?* Point out the fact that you are asking questions. Then tell the children to ask each other a question. Write some of their questions on the board, drawing attention to the question marks and why they are there. Explain that a question mark comes at the end of a sentence, replacing the full stop. Our voices change when we ask a question. You can demonstrate this by reading out a few questions and statements, emphasising the different intonation. Children need to know that a statement is a definite or clear expression of something, such as *I like chocolate*.

Activities

- **Photocopiable page 98 'Hello, Alien!'**

Introduce this activity by telling the children that an alien has just landed on Earth and that the children on the sheet are asking it questions that have got muddled. Invite the children to suggest 'wh' words which could be used to begin questions, and write them on the board. Ask the children to sort out the questions and write each one in the speech bubble. They should then think of a question that they would like to ask the alien.

- **Photocopiable page 99 'Questions and answers'**

Ask the children if the sets of words on the sheet are sentences. Can they tell you why not? At the moment, they don't make sense. Each set of words contains a question and an answer. The capital letters and question marks have been included to show where the sentences begin and where the questions end, but the children will have to make up their own minds about where to put the full stops in the answer sentences.

- **Photocopiable page 100 'The ladder'**

Talk briefly about the picture on the sheet. What do the children think is happening? Does it remind any of them of a story they know? What questions does the picture make the children want to ask? (*Where does the ladder go to? Who put it there? Why doesn't it fall down? What might happen?*) Ask the children to write four questions about the picture and then a sentence or two to say what might happen next.

Further ideas

- **Guessing game:** Hide a familiar object in a bag and invite the children to ask questions in order to find out what it is. For example: *What is it made of? How big is it?* and *Is it heavy?* Write the children's questions on the board, emphasising the question marks.
- **Finding out:** Choose a familiar character from a fairy tale. Adopt the role of that character and tell the children that they should ask you questions to find out who you are. They could ask, for example: *Did you eat porridge?* or *Are you a handsome young man?*
- **Paired work:** Ask children to write a question on a piece of paper and give it to a partner. They should then read their partner's questions and write an answer. Tell them that the question must be one to which their partner is likely to know the answer.
- **Exploring a topic:** After introducing a topic that the class are going to spend some time on, discuss with the children what they would like to know about the subject. Ask them to work in pairs or groups and to write down their questions. Share the questions with the class and write them as a list. Discuss where the children could look to find answers to their questions.

Digital content

On the digital component you will find:

- Printable versions of all three photocopiable pages.
- Answers to 'Hello, Alien!' and 'Questions and answers'.
- Interactive version of 'Hello, Alien!'.

Name:

Asking questions

Hello, Alien!

■ Make each group of words into a question and write it in a speech bubble. Write your own question in the bottom bubble.

Questions and answers

■ Rewrite these questions and answers so that they make sense. Add the full stops.

you my Have seen book?

is on table It the

____

____

____

bike? do your ride you Where

park the ride bike I in my

____

____

____

When we playground? to go can the

tea can after We go

____

____

____

Name:

Asking questions

The ladder

■ What questions would you ask about this picture?

Why ______________________

____

____

What ______________________

____

____

Where ______________________

____

Who ______________________

____

■ What do you think might happen next?

____

____

____

____

Writing and using sentences

Objective

Write and sequence sentences to form short narratives.

Background knowledge

Children will need to understand what a sentence is and how to write one; this section invites children to write their own sentences, with support. Refer to the poster 'What is a sentence?' (page 83) and talk about the different kinds of sentence. Invite children to give their own examples of statements, exclamations and questions. Children are encouraged to re-read their writing, paying attention to sentence construction and punctuation.

Activities

- **Photocopiable page 102 'A nice day out?'**
Talk through the pictures and sentences on the sheet with the children. The pictures are in order but the sentences are not. Read out the sentences, explaining that each one matches one of the first three pictures. Ask the children to join the sentence to its picture with a line and then write a sentence of their own to go with the last picture. Refer to the poster 'What is a sentence?' (page 83) and look at the different punctuation marks used to end the different types of sentence. Remind the children to use capital letters and end punctuation in their sentences.
- **Photocopiable page 103 'Clowning about'**
Discuss what is happening in each picture. Point out that some vocabulary is provided, but, together, you may want to write up some more. The children may also need help if they wish to use the verbs ('barked' and 'fell') in a different tense. However, this would be a good opportunity to remind them that most stories are told as if they happened in the past. The children should write one sentence next to each picture to tell the whole story, and then add one final sentence to continue it. Read the poster 'Check your writing' (page 84) with the children. Encourage them to re-read their work at the end and check each sentence against each point on the poster.
- **Photocopiable page 104 'Shopping'**
Explore what is happening in the picture and check that the children can read the words beneath it. Ask them to write three sentences about the picture. They can then write a sentence about something that happened when they went shopping. Remind the children to read their work to check it makes sense. They should also check that they have used capital letters and end punctuation correctly. Refer to the poster 'Check your writing' (page 84) and encourage children to use it to check their sentences after writing.

Further ideas

- **Writing about pictures:** Cover up all of the text on a Big Book page. Ask several children to say one sentence each about the illustration. Write each sentences on the board, asking all the children to tell you how to begin it and what punctuation to put at the end. Do the same with consecutive pages of the book.
- **Sharing examples:** Send pairs of children around the school, looking for examples of sentences. Ask them to note two examples and share them with the class. Is each one a sentence? Introduce the idea of 'audience'. For what audience is each of their sentences intended? (Children, visitors, parents and so on.)
- **Shared story:** Write a collaborative story and ask the children to identify sentences as you scribe. Ask them to tell you where to put the capital letters and end punctuation. Begin by providing a story starter, for example: *Yesterday in the supermarket, I saw a tiny man, no bigger than my little finger...* Tell the children to carry on with the story. Go around the class, asking each child to contribute a complete sentence. It doesn't matter if the story gets silly – the focus is on making single sentences.

Digital content

On the digital component you will find:
- Printable versions of all three photocopiable pages.
- Answers to 'A nice day out?'.
- Interactive version of 'A nice day out?'.

Name:

Writing and using sentences

A nice day out?

■ Join each sentence to one of the first three pictures with a line. Write a sentence to describe what happens in the last picture.

It rained.

We had ice cream.

We went to the park.

____

____

____

Clowning about

■ Write a sentence next to each picture to tell the story.

clown bike

dog barked

fell clown

dog bike

■ What do you think might happen next?

Name:

Writing and using sentences

Shopping

■ Write three sentences about what is happening in the picture. Then use the back of this sheet to write a sentence about a time when you went shopping.

shopping	boot	baby	car
barking	trolley	crying	dog

1. ________________________________

2. ________________________________

3. ________________________________

Chapter 5

Sentences (2)

Introduction

This chapter focuses on sentences in different genres – stories, recounts, notices, reports, poems and so on. Questions are revisited and children are asked to use the conjunctions 'and', 'but' and 'because' to join sentences.

Children should be able to tell you the words beginning with 'wh' that are often used to begin questions. Remind them that they can also make questions without these words and ask them to suggest examples. Practise changing sentences into questions. For example: *My book is on the sofa. Is my book on the sofa?* For further practice, please see the 'Sentences (2)' section of the Years 1–2 workbook.

Poster notes

Useful joining words (page 106)
Explain that simple sentences and phrases can be linked together using joining words. Invite a child to read each sentence and ask them which joining word has been used each time. Ask children to suggest different sentences using each joining word.

Types of sentence (page 107)
Explain that there are different types of sentence and share the poster with the children. Talk through the sentence types one at a time. Invite a child to read the example sentence, then challenge children to think of more examples for each sentence type. Write some of their suggestions on the board, emphasising the punctuation at the end of the sentence. For commands consider why one example sentence has an exclamation mark, while the other does not. Ensure that they understand that an exclamation mark is needed when the command is stronger or imperative.

In this chapter

Vocabulary

In Year 1 children need to know:
sentence, capital letter, full stop, question mark, exclamation mark, joining word

In Year 2 children need to know:
statement, question, exclamation, command, noun phrase

Sentences (2)

Useful joining words

We can join sentences and words to make them more interesting.

and or but

I went to the park **and** played on the swings.

You can go to the park **or** play in the garden.

I wanted to play outside **but** it was raining.

when if that because

You can have ice cream **when** you have eaten your tea.

You can buy some stickers **if** you save your pocket money.

He was unhappy **that** the teacher made him finish his work.

The dog wagged his tail **because** he was going for a walk.

Sentences (2)

Types of sentence

Statement: A sentence that tells us something.

The car is black.

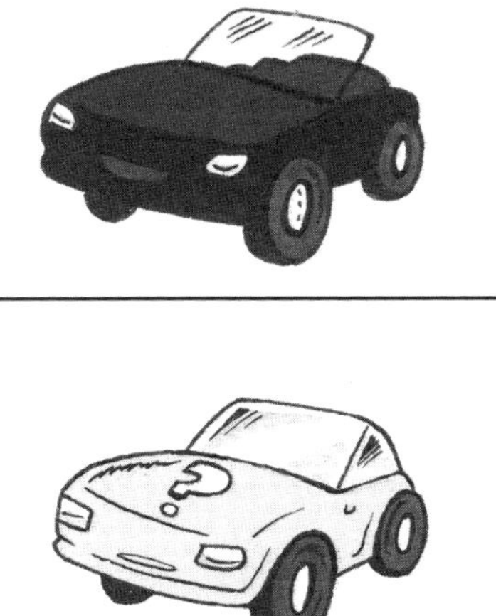

Ends with a full stop

Question: A sentence that asks something.

What colour is the car?

Ends with a question mark

Exclamation: A sentence showing surprise, shock or emotion.

What a beautiful car!

Ends with an exclamation mark

Command: A sentence that tells us to do something.

Sit in the car. Get down!

Ends with a full stop or an exclamation mark

Linking words and phrases (1)

Objective

Learn how subordinating and coordinating conjunctions can link words and phrases.

Background knowledge

Conjunctions are used to link simple sentences or phrases. A coordinating conjunction (such as *and*, *but*, *or*) links a pair of words or phrases of equal importance. For example: *They cooked tea and ate it greedily.* Subordinating conjunctions (such as *when*, *if*, *that*, *because*) link two parts of a sentence or phrases, but each part is not of equal importance. For example: *They played outside when the rain stopped.* Children should be given opportunities to use different 'joining words' to enhance their sentences. Children do not need to know the word 'conjunction' until Year 3.

Activities

- **Photocopiable page 109 'Because...'**

Talk about joining sentences using 'because'. Explain that 'because' tells you why something happened. Tell the children that each sentence on the left of the sheet can be matched with a sentence on the right. The children may have different suggestions for which sentences go together. They should join their sentences with 'because' to make new, longer sentences. They can then write their own sentence about something they dislike, using 'because' to explain why they don't like it. (Tell them that they must not name any people as the thing disliked.)

- **Photocopiable page 110 'Joining sentences'**

Explain that there are many words that can be used to join sentences or phrases. Challenge the children to match the beginnings and endings of each sentence and to link them with an appropriate joining word. Invite different children to read their sentences to the class when they have finished. Could they think of other sentences using these joining words?

- **Photocopiable page 111 'Endings'**

Introduce the children to the conjunctions 'because', 'when', 'if' and 'that'. Explain that these words can also be used to join simple sentences or phrases. Invite different children to read the sentences on the photocopiable sheet and to suggest a suitable joining word to insert in each space. Explain that it must 'make sense'. Ask children to explain their choices. Finally, tell the children to finish the sentence starters with their own endings. These can be read out to the class. Discuss whether each ending matches the conjunction that introduced it.

Further ideas

- **Finding joining words:** Find a section of a Big Book in which there are a number of conjunctions, such as 'and', 'or' and 'but', and ask the children to help you to look for them. Can they spot which two sentences are being linked?
- **Following on:** Give groups of children a sentence starter, consisting of a short sentence without the final full stop (for example, *We went for a walk*). Then give each pair within the group a different conjunction (such as 'because', 'when' 'that' and 'if'). Let the pairs make up an ending to the sentence that follows on from their conjunction. They should share them with the class and talk about whether or not the ending 'matches' the conjunction that introduced it.
- **If:** Play a round-the-class game. Start by saying: *I could be a monster if…*, adding a reason. Each child repeats the beginning and then adds their own ending. Vary by changing 'monster' to animal names or occupations, such as firefighter.

Digital content

On the digital component you will find:

- Printable versions of all three photocopiable pages.
- Answers to all three photocopiable pages.
- Interactive versions of 'Because...' and 'Endings'.

Because...

■ Each sentence on the left can be joined to one on the right using **because**. Write the new sentences you make.

I didn't go out.		He fell over.
She laughed.		The sun was shining.
He cried.	**because**	It was raining.
I was sad.		The dog got muddy.
I was happy.		I lost my teddy.

■ Finish this sentence.

I don't like ______

because ______

______.

Name:

Joining sentences

■ Choose a beginning and ending and join them with one of these words. Then write them below.

and or but

Beginning	Ending
The car spluttered	didn't win the race.
Jasmine couldn't choose between chocolate	it was closed.
Cody ran fast	goes in the car.
We went to the cafe	vanilla ice cream.
James either walks to school	ran out of petrol.

Endings

■ Choose a joining word to go in each sentence.

because	if	when	that

1. The children were finishing their work ____________ the bell rang.

2. We will have to cancel Sports Day ____________ it is raining.

3. We are tidying the classroom ____________ it is the end of term.

4. We know it is important ____________ we learn our times tables.

■ Finish these sentences.

1. The alien walked slowly up the path when

____.

2. The old lady screamed because

____.

3. The mysterious visitor would get trapped if

____.

4. The lady knew that

____.

Linking words and phrases (2)

Objective

Learn to use subordinating and coordinating conjunctions.

Background knowledge

Sentences can be simple, such as *The dog barked.* Conjunctions can extend and develop sentence writing, by enabling phrases and clauses to be joined. Different conjunctions have different roles, sometimes enabling us to add information (as in 'and') and sometimes giving contrasting information (preceded by the conjunction 'but'). The use of 'because' indicates a reason will follow. Children should be encouraged to experiment with the different functions of conjunctions in their own writing. Remember that the children are not expected to know the term 'conjunction' but may refer to these as 'joining words'.

Activities

- **Photocopiable page 113 'Home'**

Read the sentence endings with the children. Draw their attention to the joining words used beneath these: 'because', 'but' and 'when'. Ask: *Why would the word 'because' be used?* Explain that a reason or cause will follow in the second part of the sentence. When the word 'but' is used, it is followed by a contrasting reason. The word 'when' is linked to time. Challenge children to find appropriate endings for each sentence, taking care that it matches with the conjunction used. Ask them to finish by writing their own ending for the last sentence.

- **Photocopiable page 114 'Making the connection'**

Challenge the children to think of endings for each sentence beginning. Invite children to read their sentences to the class. Ask: *Does this ending match the beginning and the joining word?* Finish by asking the children to list the joining words used.

- **Photocopiable page 115 'If...'**

Encourage the children to think of adventurous or silly reasons to end each sentence. Invite children to read their sentences to the class. Discuss effective choices. Ask: *How does the word 'if' help to write the second part of the sentence?* Finish by challenging the children to write a story beginning using one of the sentences they have written. Can they find opportunities to use different joining words in their work?

Further ideas

- **Joining sentences:** Look at some examples of the children's writing. Are there places where two sentences could be linked by a joining word? Or can they think of a word to replace 'and' as a joining word?
- **Word hunt:** Ask the children to hunt for joining words when reading books, and to compile their own list. Use these words to make a class list of joining words. Encourage the children to refer to and use these words in their own writing. Discuss the contribution these words make to their writing.

Digital content

On the digital component you will find:
- Printable versions of all three photocopiable pages.
- Answers to 'Home'.

Home

■ Use these sentences to finish each sentence below.

I wasn't tired.	It was late.
I didn't go to bed.	It was getting dark.
School had finished.	It was tea-time.

1. We went home because

____.

2. We went home because

____.

3. We went home but

____.

4. We went home but

____.

5. We went home when

____.

6. We went home when

____.

■ Write your own ending.

7. I ate breakfast but

____

____

Name:

Linking words and phrases (2)

Making the connection

■ Finish these sentences.

1. I'm missing playtime because

______________________________.

2. I told you to write a story but

______________________________.

3. My old bike broke when

______________________________.

4. I can sneak out if

______________________________.

5. I could eat you or

______________________________.

6. I'll cast a spell on you that

______________________________.

7. I like doing silly things and

______________________________.

■ List the words that join the first part of each sentence to your added words.

Joining words:

____

____

Name:

Linking words and phrases (2)

If...

■ Finish these sentences.

1. I could be an astronaut if

____.

2. I could travel on a magic carpet if

____.

3. I could walk with dinosaurs if

____.

4. I could explore a rainforest if

____.

■ Choose one of the ideas above and write a story beginning.

■ Try to use these joining words:

and but because when if

____

____

____

____

____

Different kinds of sentence

Objective

Understand and distinguish between the different functions of sentences.

Background knowledge

Children need to know and recognise different kinds of sentence. Statements are sentences that impart information and end with a full stop. For example, *The cat sat on the mat.* is a statement, as it tells us what the cat is doing. The sentence *Where is the cat?* is asking us about the cat and so is a question. *What a big cat!* is an exclamation, expressing surprise at the cat's size. It ends with an exclamation mark. Commands can end with a full stop or an exclamation mark. A command that is asking someone to do something, such as *Please wash up.*, does not need an exclamation mark. A more extreme command should have an exclamation mark, such as *Stop!*

Activities

- **Photocopiable page 117 'Asking or telling?'**

Start by referring to the poster 'Types of sentence' (page 107). Ask: *What is a statement? What is a question?* Ensure that children understand the differences between both types of sentence and are able to give examples of both. Explain that in this activity some of the sentences are questions, but the question marks have been left off. Remind them to look for 'question words' to help them find the questions. The children should finish these statements and questions by adding the appropriate punctuation. As an extension, they can give their own final question to a partner and answer theirs, remembering to use a capital letter and full stop.

- **Photocopiable page 118 'What is it? (2)'**

Refer to the poster 'Types of sentence' (page 107). Invite the children to give their own examples of a statement, a question and a command. Introduce the sheet and ask children to draw lines to match each sentence with the sentence type labels at the top. Challenge them to write a sentence for each type. Finish by sharing sentences and discuss whether each one matches the correct sentence type.

- **Photocopiable page 119 'Exclamations and commands'**

Explain that exclamations are expressions of strong feelings, often of surprise, fear or anger. Invite the children to give examples of exclamations. Tell the children that there are two types of command. The first is when someone tells you to do something and would not need an exclamation mark at the end, such as *Close your books*. A stronger command, which requires immediate obedience, would need an exclamation mark, such as *Stop that!* Ask children to give examples of both types, before inviting them to match the sentences to the appropriate box. Finish by asking them to write their own exclamations and commands.

Further ideas

- **Book search:** Give each child a book. Ask them to find three statements and three questions and write them down. Encourage the children to share their findings with a partner.
- **Labels:** Ask the children to write labels for commands needed in the classroom. Challenge them to decide which labels need an exclamation mark and which ones do not.
- **Dog trainer:** Challenge the children to create a poster showing a list of commands that could be used in dog training. Encourage them to punctuate the commands with exclamation marks.

Digital content

On the digital component you will find:

- Printable versions of all three photocopiable pages.
- Answers to all three photocopiable pages.
- Interactive versions of all three photocopiable pages.

Asking or telling?

■ Decide which of these are questions and which are statements. Add the missing full stops and question marks.

Was the dog in the snow

Was he cold

This is my house

Do you want a pizza

This is my book

What do you want to do

Let's all go out to play

Do you want to go home

■ Write a question of your own and ask a friend to write an answer.

Question: ______________________________

____

Answer: ______________________________

Name:

Different kinds of sentence

What is it? (2)

■ Draw lines to connect these sentences to the correct types. Some have been done for you.

Go away!

Here's a ball.

Here's your ball.

Sit!

command (!)

statement (.)

question (?)

Where are you?

I'm in bed

What are you doing?

Come!

Watch out!

■ Write a sentence for each sentence type.

1. Write a question:

____

2. Write a statement:

____

3. Write a command:

____

Exclamations and commands

■ Join each sentence to the correct box.

1. What a beautiful day!
2. Come here!
3. Please tidy up.
4. It's spoiled!
5. Go to bed!

Exclamation
Showing surprise, anger or strong feelings. It starts with a capital letter and ends with an exclamation mark.

Command
Telling someone do something. It starts with a capital letter and ends with a full stop or an exclamation mark.

■ Write a command for a dog.

___

■ Write a command for your teacher.

___

■ Write an exclamation for opening a present.

___

Improving your writing

Objective

Learn how to use expanded noun phrases.

Background knowledge

A noun phrase is a group of words that contain a noun. It is a phrase with a noun as its head, such as *some children*, *happy children* and *three happy children*. Using noun phrases in a sentence can add interest and detail to a simple sentence. So *The cat sat on the mat* can become *The fluffy cat sat on the red mat*. At this stage inserting adjectives before a noun will create simple and effective noun phrases. An expanded noun phrase can use more than one adjective, as in *The fluffy black cat*. Using adjectives before nouns adds more precision to our writing and is a basic skill in description.

Activities

- **Photocopiable page 121 'Noun phrase hunt'**
Write *The cat sat on the mat*. on the board. Explain that this is a simple sentence, but we can add adjectives before each noun to make it more interesting. Invite suggestions from the children and write them down. Explain that an adjective and a noun together create a noun phrase. Using noun phrases makes sentences more interesting. Challenge the children to find the noun phrases in each sentence on the photocopiable sheet. Finish by asking them to rewrite some sentences using noun phrases. Share the children's sentences.
- **Photocopiable page 122 'Word sums'**
Explain that they should combine an adjective and a noun to make a noun phrase. Invite children to give examples. When the children have finished, share their noun phrases and discuss which are most effective. Challenge the children to choose one of their noun phrases and to use it in a sentence. How did it improve the sentence?
- **Photocopiable page 123 'Make a noun phrase'**
Invite different children to read out the nouns and adjectives. Discuss the meaning of any unfamiliar adjectives. Ask the children to work with a partner to cut out the word cards and to make two piles. They should then take an adjective card and a noun card and combine them to make a noun phrase, which they read to a partner. Challenge the children to make up a simple story using their noun phrases.

Further ideas

- **Alphabet animals:** Start by saying an adjective and an animal both beginning with 'a', for example: *amazing ant*. The next child should then suggest an adjective and animal both beginning with 'b'. Work around the class, going through the alphabet. Children could make a dictionary containing all the animals.
- **Big Book:** When reading a shared story, invite children to find noun phrases. Write down interesting noun phrases, so children can use them in their own writing. Challenge children to suggest different noun phrases to substitute those they have found.

Digital content

On the digital component you will find:

- Printable versions of all three photocopiable pages.
- Answers to 'Noun phrase hunt'.
- Interactive version of 'Noun phrase hunt'.

Improving your writing

Noun phrase hunt

■ Underline the noun phrase in each sentence.

1. The beautiful princess slept on and on.
2. They walked through the gloomy forest.
3. They counted more than a thousand people.
4. The exciting story had entertained everyone.
5. The big red balloon floated upwards.
6. The enormous hairy monster plodded towards us.

■ Rewrite these sentences using a noun phrase.

1. The dog panted.

____

2. They arrived at the castle.

____

3. The baby was crying.

____

Name:

Improving your writing

Word sums

Adjective + **Noun** = **Noun phrase**

↑ big ↑ dog ↑ big dog

Adjective	Noun
enormous	crocodile
creepy	present
amazing	garden
delightful	castle
spiky	monster
terrible	forest
green	lake

- Choose adjectives and nouns to make four noun phrases.

- Use one of your noun phrases in a sentence.

Improving your writing

Make a noun phrase

- Cut out the cards.
- Make a pile of nouns and a pile of adjectives.
- Choose an adjective and a noun.
- Read the noun phrase to a partner.
- Can you use your noun phrases to make up a story to tell your partner?

castle	river	house
snake	giant	witch
girl	boy	cave
dinosaur	cottage	bear
fierce	slithery	terrifying
winding	crooked	young
gentle	ruined	charming
gloomy	quaint	enormous

Different types of writing

Objective

Write for different purposes.

Background knowledge

Children should be given experience of writing for different purposes. They need to write narratives about real and fictional experiences (of themselves and others), write poetry and write about real events. Look at a variety of text types with the children and point out that, although the layout may be different, they are all made up of sentences that begin with capital letters and end with full stops, question marks or exclamation marks. Help them to see that while stories and recounts usually use the past tense, information texts are often in the present tense.

Activities

- **Photocopiable page 125 'The Gingerbread Man'** Talk through the pictures to tell the story of 'The Gingerbread Man'. You may like to write some useful vocabulary on the board. Ask the children to write a sentence next to each picture on the sheet to describe what is happening. Explain that the aim is to tell the story in four sentences. Encourage more confident children to go back and write a second sentence about each picture.
- **Photocopiable page 126 'What do they say?'** Show children the pictures of the characters. Ask the children to tell you who each character is. Invite them to discuss with a partner what each character could be saying. Remind them how to write an exclamation or command. You may wish to provide some useful vocabulary on the board. Challenge children to write an exclamation or command in the speech bubble for each character. Share children's writing at the end. Encourage more confident children to draw their own character and write an exclamation on the back of the sheet.
- **Photocopiable page 127 'All about dinosaurs'** Show the children a picture of a dinosaur. Explain that they should describe the dinosaur, using expanded noun phrases to make the description more interesting. Invite different children to say a sentence about different parts of its body. Ask: *Can anyone think of a different noun phrase to describe that?* When the children have completed their descriptions, invite some to read them out. Compare the effectiveness of different sentences.

Further ideas

- **Shared writing:** If you have Big Books that contain different types of text, for example, instructions, a report or an explanation, stick large pieces of paper over the text. With the children, write your own text on the paper, asking them to create a new sentence for every page.
- **Fact finding:** Ask the children to choose a simple non-fiction book to look through. They should write down a question, the answer to which they know can be found in the book. They then give the book and the question to a partner. Explain that, if it is a long book, they should tell their partner on which page or in which section the answer can be found.
- **Opposites:** Choose a passage from a book containing description and expanded noun phrases. Challenge the children to read a sentence, changing noun phrases so they have the opposite meaning, for example *huge* becomes *tiny*.

Digital content

On the digital component you will find:

- Printable versions of all three photocopiable pages.

Name:

Different types of writing

The Gingerbread Man

■ Tell the story by writing a sentence for each picture. Use the words from the bottom of the page.

Gingerbread Man
oven ran away

Name:

Different types of writing

What do they say?

■ Write an exclamation or command for each character.

SCHOLASTIC
www.scholastic.co.uk

Name:

Different types of writing

All about dinosaurs

- Describe a dinosaur, using expanded noun phrases.
- Think about the dinosaur's:

head legs arms tail
body mouth teeth skin

Useful adjectives:

straight sharp enormous powerful
terrible spiky massive skinny
fierce short long

Chapter 6

Punctuating sentences

Introduction

The most basic punctuation is that used to demarcate sentences – the capital letter at the beginning and the full stop, question mark or exclamation mark at the end. Once children have grasped this they can start looking at punctuation that divides up the sentence, such as the use of commas. For further practice, please see the 'Punctuating sentences' section of the Years 1–2 workbook.

Poster notes

Punctuation (page 129)

The poster demonstrates how to use the full stop, question mark, exclamation mark and comma. Can the children tell you why an exclamation mark and a question mark have been used? Point out the punctuation in the last sentence; explain that the comma is used to show the separate items in the list. It also tells the reader how to read the sentence.

Using apostrophes (page 130)

This poster shows how to use an apostrophe for contractions and to show possession. Explain to the children that we often join words to make one word. We use the apostrophe to show where letters have been missed out. Explain that when something belongs to a person, place or object we need to use an apostrophe and 's' to show possession. Invite children to write their own examples. For nouns ending in 's', use words such as *James*, *bus* and *class*.

In this chapter

Vocabulary

In Year 1 children need to know:
full stop, capital letter, sentence, question mark, exclamation mark, punctuation

In Year 2 children need to know:
comma, apostrophe, joining words

Punctuating sentences

Punctuation

Capital letter T

There was a spooky castle.

Full stop .

The children saw something large and hairy.

Exclamation mark !

Look at that! It's enormous.

Question mark ?

What is it? Is it a monster?

Comma ,

Does it have legs, ears and a tail?

Punctuating sentences

Using apostrophes

to join words	
I am	I'm
I have	I've
she is	she's
we have	we've
they are	they're
cannot	can't
did not	didn't
was not	wasn't
were not	weren't
could not	couldn't

to show ownership by one thing

noun doesn't end in 's'

add apostrophe and **s**

For example:

Sam in *Sam's dog*

dog in *dog's lead*

noun ends in 's'

add apostrophe and **s**

For example:

Paris in *Paris's tower*

princess in *princess's dress*

Sentence punctuation

Objective

Begin to punctuate sentences using a capital letter and a full stop, question mark or exclamation mark.

Background knowledge

The sentence is the basic unit of language, but sentences can be very varied. The more they read, the more children will become aware of the possibilities available, and this can be made explicit to them during shared reading sessions. Make clear to the children that punctuation helps to make the meaning of a sentence. It is not just a matter of putting it in at the end to please the teacher. For this reason, it is important to teach punctuation in relation to meaning. A capital letter is not a punctuation mark but its function in starting a sentence is taught at the same time as the full stop. It is important that as each punctuation mark is introduced to the children, its function is explained and explored. As children gain greater control over punctuating sentences in their writing, they will be able to communicate their ideas more effectively.

Activities

- **Photocopiable page 132 'A fine fish'**

On this sheet, a variety of sentences have been written without capital letters or full stops. Write a similar 'wrong' sentence on the board (for example: *my dog is hungry*). Tell the children to correct the sentences on the sheet by sticking the capital letters over the appropriate lower-case letters and then adding full stops.

- **Photocopiable page 133 'Fish and cats and dogs'**

Tell the children that none of the sentences on the sheet are finished and that you want them to complete them with the appropriate punctuation. Advise the children that, as they use each punctuation mark, they can cross it off at the bottom of the page.

- **Photocopiable page 134 'Catch!'**

Ask the children to practise reading these sentences aloud in different ways. Which ones would they normally say in a loud voice? Tell them to choose whether to put a full stop or an exclamation mark at the end of every sentence. Then ask the children to work in pairs, each taking a role and reading the words aloud. Advise them to think how the characters would say the words and what tells them about the punctuation needed. Is it a question, a statement or an exclamation? When the children have added the punctuation, they should read the dialogue aloud again and ask themselves if it sounds right. Remind them to consider the punctuation.

Further ideas

- **Insert the punctuation:** Find a passage from a story with which the children are familiar, preferably one that has question marks and/or exclamation marks in it. Write the text, leaving out the punctuation, then ask the children to tell you what punctuation is missing and to help you insert it. Invite them to check the new punctuation against the original. Do they differ?
- **Making up sentences:** Children could write down three words each and swap them with a partner. Each child then has to make up a sentence using the words they have been given. This exercise could also be used to make questions.
- **Quiz:** Ask groups of children to devise a quiz for another group. They can write ten questions, making sure that each one ends with a question mark.

Digital content

On the digital component you will find:

- Printable versions of all three photocopiable pages.
- Answers to all three photocopiable pages.
- Interactive versions of all three photocopiable pages.

Name:

Sentence punctuation

A fine fish

■ Cut out the capital letters and stick them in the right places. Add the full stops.

i am hungry

this is my sandwich

look at this fish

put on your boots

i want something to eat

we went swimming

i can see you

we can play in the park

W

Name:

Sentence punctuation

Fish and cats and dogs

■ Add the four full stops and four question marks in the correct places.

That girl had a fish

What day is it

I am at home

Do you want a sweet

I like the black cat

Is Dad at home

I want a sandwich

Is that his dog

. . ? ?

. ? ?

.

Name:

Sentence punctuation

Catch!

■ Put in the full stops and exclamation marks.

Look out ☐

I am looking for my gloves ☐

Go away ☐

I hate spiders ☐

He is watching TV ☐

■ Put these punctuation marks in the right places.

! ! ? ? ? . .

Come and play ☐

What do you want to play ☐

Can we play catch ☐

Yes. Here's a ball ☐

Can you catch this ☐

Watch out ☐

Help ☐

Using sentence punctuation

Objective

Use familiar punctuation correctly.

Background knowledge

The items of punctuation covered in these activities are the capital letter, the full stop, the question mark and exclamation mark. (The capital letter is, strictly speaking, not a punctuation mark, but is taught at the same time as the full stop.) Punctuation emerges through children's writing as it develops. Children will often write sentences that should include certain items of punctuation but omit the actual marks. The emphasis here is on activities that help to draw out the individual child's awareness of punctuation.

Activities

- **Photocopiable page 136 'Oops!'**

Discuss the actions in the pictures and make sure that the children can read the words next to each one. Ask them to write a different type of sentence next to each picture to describe what is happening. Remind them that each sentence should start with a capital letter, but should end with either a full stop, a question mark or an exclamation mark, to match the type of sentence. They can then write one or two sentences of their own about an accident that happened to them or to someone they know. They can swap their work with that of a partner and use the checklist on the poster 'Punctuation' (page 129) to check that they have used end punctuation and capital letters correctly.

- **Photocopiable page 137 'Check these out'**

The sentences provided in this activity will accommodate the use of capital letters, full stops, question marks and an exclamation mark.

- **Photocopiable page 138 'Recycle the words'**

This activity gives children the opportunity to devise sentences of their own. The words in the bins can be used to produce examples of punctuated sentences.

Invite the children to tell you whether each sentence is a statement, a question or an exclamation. Can they explain why? The children should consider the various types of demarcation they can use. Compare the results to see how children used their words.

Further ideas

- **Punctuation finding:** Invite children to look through texts to find the different types of punctuation used. Can they figure out from these contexts the functions of various punctuation marks?
- **Question setting:** Children can 'hot-seat' by setting their own questions for others in the class to answer. Ask questions such as: *What are your favourite colours?* and *Where did you go last weekend?* Establish a questions board for children to pin on questions that they would like to ask a member of the class. A variation of this activity is to ask children to look at the board and answer a chosen number of questions that it poses.
- **Recycles:** Photocopiable page 138 'Recycle the words' can be adapted to use a new set of words. This can work well if vocabulary from a particular topic is included (such as science: *gravity*, *force*). Children can then use their developing subject knowledge to devise a set of questions.

Digital content

On the digital component you will find:

- Printable versions of all three photocopiable pages.
- Answers to 'Check these out'.
- Interactive version of 'Check these out'.

Name:

Using sentence punctuation

Oops!

■ Write three sentences about the pictures below, saying what happened. Use a full stop, an exclamation mark and a question mark.

■ Start each sentence with a capital letter.

doll dropped pond

fell boy scooter

let go kite

■ What else happened?

Name:

Using sentence punctuation

Check these out

■ Rewrite these sentences with the correct punctuation.

1. i can see my friend

____

2. can we go to the park

____

3. is it raining

____

4. we are going to the park

____

5. what a beautiful flower

____

6. can you see my friend

____

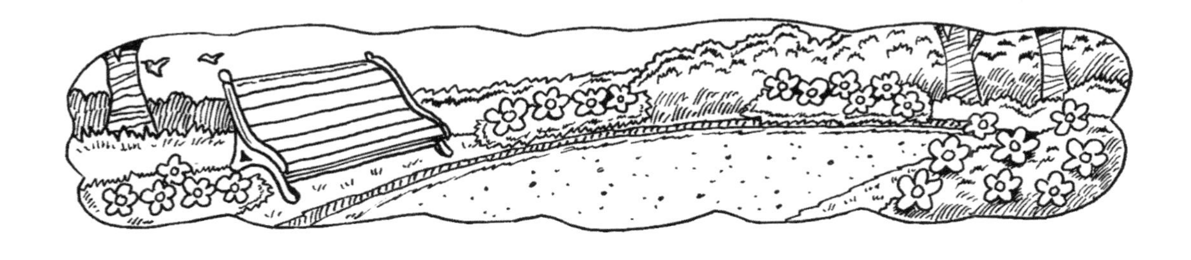

Name:

Using sentence punctuation

Recycle the words

■ These words have been thrown away. Can you use the words in each bin to make a new sentence? Say each sentence aloud then write some of them down.

More capital letters

Objective

Use a capital letter for names of people, places, the days of the week and the personal pronoun.

Background knowledge

Common nouns are general names for things. For example, in the sentence *I fed the dog*, the noun 'dog' could be used to refer to any dog, not to a specific one. Children should recognise that some nouns are special, and that to show they are special we begin them with capital letters. These words – which identify specific things or people – are proper nouns. In a phrase such as *Jess is my dog* the word 'dog' is the common noun; 'Jess' is a proper noun because it refers to and identifies a specific dog. Names of places, such as *London* or *England* are also proper nouns. Days of the week and months of the year are also proper nouns and begin with a capital letter. Chapter 1, Section 3 introduces proper nouns and should be covered before using material in this section.

Activities

- **Photocopiable page 140 'The magic bus'**

Tell the children that they are going to write a story about a journey on a magic bus. Ask them where they would like to go if a magic bus picked them up. Write some of the place names they suggest, prompting them to tell what you should put at the beginning of the words. Read through the activity together, pointing out the commas that will separate their lists of people and place names. When they have completed the sentences, they can continue the story.

- **Photocopiable page 141 'On holiday'**

Tell the children to imagine that they sent this postcard while on holiday in Spain, but that they have left out nearly all the capital letters. Read the text through to the children, and ask them to correct it. Advise them to look for the beginnings of sentences and put in the capital letters there, then find 'special' words (proper nouns) and give them capitals. Remind children that 'I' always has a capital letter and that days of the week are proper nouns and also need to start with a capital letter. Next ask the children to imagine that they have sent this card to school. Ask them to write the school name and address on the right-hand side of the postcard, using capital letters as appropriate.

- **Photocopiable page 142 'The giant of Biggin Hill'**

Read through the sheet together and tell the children to look out for the names of people and places. Explain that they should cross out the initial letter and write a capital above it. They should also put capitals at the beginning of sentences. Point out that the title needs correcting too. Ask the children to make a list of the people and places mentioned. The children can then continue the story, using the back of the sheet.

Further ideas

- **Checking:** Ask children to look through some recent examples of their own writing, looking for the names of special places and people. Did they begin these naming words with capital letters?
- **Examples:** Ask children to look around the classroom and the school for examples of words that begin with capital letters. They should share their findings with the rest of the class and discuss why capital letters have been used in each case.
- **Diary:** Ask the children to write each day of the week in order, allowing space between each one. They can then, during the next week, write a few sentences, describing something they have done on each day. Ensure that children use capital letters to start each day of the week.

Digital content

On the digital component you will find:

- Printable versions of all three photocopiable pages.
- Answers to 'On holiday' and 'The giant of Biggin Hill'.
- Interactive version of 'On holiday'.

Name:

More capital letters

The magic bus

■ Write the names of the people who went on the bus and the places it went to. Remember to include capital letters.

I went on a magic bus.

I took four people with me.

They were ______________________, ______________________,

______________________ and ______________________ .

The bus set off.

We went to four places.

We went to ______________________, ______________________,

______________________ and ______________________ .

We stopped at ______________________ and we all got out. Then we had a big surprise.

■ What happened next?

____

____

____

____

Name:

More capital letters

On holiday

- Read the postcard. Find the words with the missing capital letters and correct them.
- Write your school's address in the space.

Hello everyone
we are on holiday in spain.
dan and i are having a great
time. we went swimming on
sunday.
we will see you soon.
Best wishes
Kim

Name:

More capital letters

The giant of Biggin Hill

■ Put capital letters in the right places and continue the story. Remember to use capital letters and full stops.

once there was a giant called max. he lived on biggin hill in upland. max had a dog called kelly, but he had no friends.

a young girl called eliza lived nearby. she lived with her three little brothers.

every day, eliza cleaned the house and fed the animals. she worked hard and max felt sorry for her.

one day, ______________________________

____

____

____

____

____

____

Commas in lists

Objective

Use commas to separate items in a list.

Background knowledge

Draw a comma on the board and explain that it is a punctuation mark called a comma. Explain that it can be used to separate items in a list. Write an example sentence, such as: *I went shopping and bought apples, bananas, grapes and oranges.* Read it aloud. Then read it aloud again, asking the children to notice where you pause. Children should understand how commas help when reading lists aloud, by indicating pauses. Point out the commas and explain that they tell you how to read the sentence and, in this way, they help to make the meaning clear. Write another, similar sentence, omitting the commas. Read the sentence aloud and ask children to tell you where to put the commas. In all the activities in this section, encourage the children to read out their completed sentences, taking account of the commas by pausing. Ensure that children understand that a comma is not usually used before the word 'and' in a list.

Activities

- **Photocopiable page 144 'What I like'**
Ask the children what they like to have for lunch at school. Write their suggestions in sentences on the board, using commas to separate the items. Point out that there is no comma between the last items linked by 'and'. The children may suggest items that are more than one word, such as cheese sandwiches or orange juice. Demonstrate that the comma comes after the complete item, not after each word, and write an example on the board.
- **Photocopiable page 145 'What you need (1)'**
This activity and the one on page 146 focus on the types of list that occur in instructional texts. Write the heading *You will need:* on the board. Underneath, in a column, write a list of ingredients, for example *eggs, flour* and *milk*. Ask the children where they would see this type of list. (In a recipe, perhaps – show the children some similar lists in a cookery book.) Explain that these lists could be written as sentences and rewrite them together, using commas. Tell them that they should decide which list is required for each activity. Point out that 'suntan lotion' is one item and that the comma should go after 'lotion'.
- **Photocopiable page 146 'What you need (2)'**
In this activity, children must decide for themselves how to punctuate the list. Remind them that they do not need a comma when two items are separated by the word 'and'. As an extension, you could make available some cookery books or books of instructions of how to make or do things. Ask the children to rewrite some of the lists of 'What you need' as sentences, using commas to separate the items.

Further ideas

- **Writing lists:** Ask the children to help you write a list of things you need if you go to stay with a friend or relative overnight – pyjamas, toothbrush and so on. They can then write a sentence of their own, punctuated with commas, listing the things they need on the board, emphasising the question marks.
- **Ideal school:** Make a class book about your school, using sentences in which items are separated by commas. The children could list things that are good about the school and those that could be improved. Alternatively, ask them to describe their ideal school, listing all of its attributes in sentences. For example: *My ideal school would have a swimming pool, a full-sized football pitch, a zoo and a flower garden.*

Digital content

On the digital component you will find:
- Printable versions of all three photocopiable pages.

Name:

Commas in lists

What I like

■ Finish these sentences. Then colour over the commas.

For lunch I like ______________, ______________,

______________ and ______________.

For tea I like ______________, ______________,

______________ and ______________.

Some things I don't like to eat are ______________,

______________, ______________ and

______________.

Some people I like are ______________,

______________, ______________ and

______________.

Some colours I like are ______________,

______________, ______________ and

______________.

Commas in lists

What you need (1)

■ Use each of these lists to finish one of the sentences. The items listed can appear in any order in the sentence.

suntan lotion	gloves	butter	tomatoes
a towel	a coat	flour	cucumber
a bucket	a scarf	eggs	lettuce
a spade	a hat	sugar	celery

To go out in the winter you need

________________, ________________,

________________ and ________________.

To go to the beach you need ________________,

________________, ________________ and

________________.

To make a cake you need ________________,

________________, ________________ and

________________.

To make a salad you need ________________,

________________, ________________ and

________________.

Name:

Commas in lists

What you need (2)

■ Use these lists to finish the sentences. The items listed can appear in any order in the sentence.

bread	paper	a cage	glasses
butter	sticky tape	straw	knives
cheese	scissors	food	forks
	ribbon	water	spoons
		a bowl	plates

To wrap a present you need ______________________________

____.

To set the table you need ______________________________

____.

To keep a hamster you need ______________________________

____.

To make a cheese sandwich you need ______________________

____.

Apostrophes for missing letters

Objective

Use apostrophes for contracted forms.

Background knowledge

Apostrophes can mark possession. At this stage children are introduced to possession for single nouns only and are shown how to add an apostrophe and 's' to both nouns that don't end with 's' and those that do end with 's'. Apostrophes can also mark the contraction of a word or words. They show where two words have been contracted together with some of the letters removed, marking the point at which the letters once stood – so 'did not', for example, loses the 'o' to become 'didn't'. Children should be introduced to the term 'apostrophe' in Year 2 and need to know that it can be used to join words, shows where letters have been omitted (contraction), and also shows possession (see page 151).

Activities

- **Photocopiable page 148 'About us'**

Draw an apostrophe on the board. Explain that apostrophes are used to show letters have been missed out. Write *I am* on the board. Invite the children to tell you how this can be shortened. Demonstrate how this is written, using an apostrophe: *I'm.* Ask the children to tell you which letter has been missed out. Challenge the children to match the words with the contractions. When they have done this, go through each one and invite children to tell you which letters have been missed out. Finish by asking the children to write the contractions for words in bold. Remind them that the apostrophe is used to show where letters have been missed out.

- **Photocopiable page 149 'Joining words'**

Ask the children to match the joined words with their originals and to write them down. Remind the children to add the apostrophe to show where letters have been missed out. Invite different children to read each contraction and tell you which letters have been missed out. Go round the class asking different children to orally put each contraction into a sentence.

- **Photocopiable page 150 'Which one?'**

Some contractions can represent more than one combination of words. This activity focuses on *it's* and *he'd* and looks at the different combinations for each. Encourage children to read the sentences and insert the correct combination, checking it makes sense. Challenge children to use each contraction in a sentence, which they can share with the class.

Further ideas

- **Contraction hunt:** Ask the children to list any new contractions they find in their own reading or in conversations. This can then form the basis of a discussion to work out what the original words are. Some contractions may be localised, such as *ain't* instead of *isn't*.
- **Redrafting:** Encourage children to review their own writing to see where they could have used apostrophes for joining words. Ensure they use the apostrophe in the correct place.
- **Joining words game:** Ask the children to make cards for ten contractions. They should then make a card for the matching words for each contraction. They should give the two piles of cards to a partner, who can then match them.

Digital content

On the digital component you will find:

- Printable versions of all three photocopiable pages.
- Answers to all three photocopiable pages.
- Interactive versions of all three photocopiable pages.

Name:

Apostrophes for missing letters

About us

■ Match these words to the correct word with an apostrophe.

I am	she's
I will	I'm
I have	she'll
she is	I'll
she will	she hasn't
she has not	I've

■ Join the words **in bold** using an apostrophe.

He is playing football.

They will come for tea

I have learned my tables.

Joining words

Apostrophes are used to join words together. The apostrophe shows us where letters have been missed out.

did not → **didn't**

o missed out

- Write the joined words next to their original words.

we've	cannot	______
couldn't	it is	______
didn't	it has	______
I'm	did not	______
isn't	could not	______
you'll	I will	______
it's	I am	______
can't	you will	______
I'll	is not	______
it's	we have	______

Name:

Apostrophes for missing letters

Which one?

it's = it is **or** it has
he'd = he had **or** he would **or** he could

■ Write the correct one under the word in bold.

It's been snowing all day.

Now **it's** stopped raining, we can go out.

When **it's** time to go home, the bell will ring.

My dad said **he'd** meet me from school.

Jack said **he'd** brought some stickers to school.

Mr Thomas said **he'd** referee the match.

■ Use **it's** in a sentence.

■ Use **he'd** in a sentence.

Apostrophes for belonging

Objective

Use apostrophes to mark singular possession in nouns.

Background knowledge

Apostrophes can be used to show possession. Although children are introduced to apostrophes for possession in Year 2 and need to know the term 'apostrophe', they are not introduced to the term 'possession'. You may wish to talk about objects 'belonging to' to the preceding nouns. An apostrophe in a noun shows the following item belongs to it (is possessed by it), such as *Sean's book*. Rules for adding apostrophes depend on the nouns to which they are being added.

- **If the noun is singular and does not end in 's':** add an apostrophe and an 's', for example: *Sam's dog* and *Kate's football.*
- **If the noun is singular and does end in 's':** add an apostrophe and an 's', for example: *Ross's cat* and *Paris's tower.*

Activities

- **Photocopiable page 152 'It's mine!'**

Refer to the poster 'Using apostrophes' (page 130), looking at the section on apostrophes for possession, focusing particularly on people's names. Explain that if something belongs to a person, we use an apostrophe and 's' to show that. Write a child's name on the board and the word 'pencil', for example, *Ahmed pencil.* Explain that the pencil belongs to Ahmed, so we put an apostrophe after his name and an 's' to show this (demonstrate it). Ask the children to write their name with the word 'pencil'. Can they put the apostrophe and 's' in the correct place?

- **Photocopiable page 153 'Belonging'**

Remind the children that apostrophes are used to show an object belongs to something or someone. It shows that an object belongs to a noun. Point to a child's jumper. Say: *The jumper belongs to the girl/boy. How can I use an apostrophe to show that?* Invite a child to write: *the boy/girl's jumper.* Explain that the apostrophe and 's' go after the noun. Challenge the children to work through the sheet making sure that the apostrophe and 's' are in the correct place.

- **Photocopiable page 154 'Who do I belong to?'**

The focus on this activity is adding apostrophe and 's' to nouns ending in 's'. Explain that the rule is the same. Keep the original word or name and just add 's'. Refer to the poster 'Using apostrophes' (page 130) and invite children to read the examples of words and names ending in 's'. Ask children to complete the activity, first writing the matching phrases with an apostrophe and 's'. Finally, ask children to read the sentences and to fill in the missing words to say what belongs to whom.

Further ideas

- **Contraction hunt:** Ask the children to list any new contractions they find in their own reading or in conversations. This can then form the basis of a discussion to work out what the original words are.
- **Book search:** Challenge children to search through a book to find examples of apostrophes being used to show objects belonging to people or things. Write down their findings and discuss the use of the apostrophe in each one. Can they think of their own examples of phrases that use apostrophes to show belonging?
- **All around us:** Ask children to make a list of apostrophes they see on shop signs and notices. Share their findings and ask the children if all the apostrophes are used correctly. Are there any apostrophes that are not used as they would expect? At this stage, children have not been shown how to use apostrophes with plural nouns, so brief reference may need to be made to this.

Digital content

On the digital component you will find:

- Printable versions of all three photocopiable pages.
- Answers to all three photocopiable pages.
- Interactive versions of 'It's mine'.

Name:

Apostrophes for belonging

It's mine!

The apostrophe shows **the dog belongs to Sam**.

Look at Sam's dog.

Apostrophe + s shows something belongs to a person.

■ Use an apostrophe for these. The first one has been done for you.

Apostrophes for belonging

Belonging

The collar belongs to the dog.
Use an apostrophe: **the dog's collar**

's after the word **dog**

- Try adding apostrophes to these.

1. The bottle belongs to the baby.

____

2. The book belongs to school.

____

3. The wheels belong to the car.

____

4. The trousers belong to the boy.

____

5. The rubber belongs to the girl.

____

Name:

Apostrophes for belonging

Who do I belong to?

Look at these nouns ending with 's':

The car belongs to Thomas. **Thomas's car**

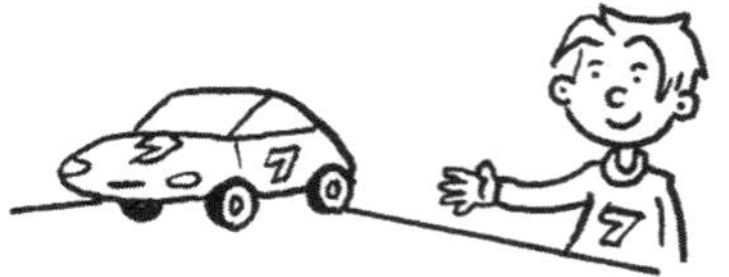

's after **Thomas**

The fish belong to the class. **The class's fish**

's after **class**

- Now try adding apostrophes to these.

1. The driver belongs to the bus. ______________________

2. The cards belong to James. ______________________

3. The computer belongs to my boss. ______________________

- Finish these sentences.

1. We went up Paris's Eiffel Tower.

The ________________ belongs to ________________ .

2. We all enjoyed hearing about Tess's dog.

The ________________ belongs to ________________ .

3. We have performed Mr Jones's play.

The ________________ belongs to ________________ .

4. The cross's wood needed painting.

The ________________ belongs to ________________ .

Subject knowledge

1. Preliminary notes about grammar

Grammar involves the way in which words of different types are combined into sentences. The explanatory sections that follow will include definitions of types of word along with notes on how they are combined into sentences.

Three preliminary points about grammar:

- Function is all-important. Where a word is placed in relation to another word is crucial in deciding whether it is functioning as a verb or a noun. For example, the word 'run' will often be thought of as a verb. However, in a sentence like *They went for a run*, the word functions as a noun and the verb is 'went'.
- There are some consistencies in the way spelling is linked to grammar. For example, words like 'play' and 'shout' have the 'ed' ending to make past tense verbs, 'played' and 'shouted'. Adjectives like 'quick' and 'slow' take a 'ly' ending to make adverbs like 'quickly' and 'slowly'. There are exceptions to these rules but such consistencies can still prove useful when it comes to understanding the grammar of sentences.
- Nothing is sacred in language. Rules change over time; the double negative has gained currency, and regional variation in accent and dialect is now far more valued than has been the case in the past. The rules of grammar that follow are subject to change as the language we use lives and grows.

2. Words and functions

Grammar picks out the functions of words. The major classes or types of word in the English language are:

Noun

The name of something or someone, including concrete things, such as 'dog' or 'tree', and abstract things, such as 'happiness' or 'fear'.

Pronoun

A word that replaces a noun. The noun 'John' in *John is ill* can be replaced by a pronoun 'he', making *He is ill*.

Verb

A word that denotes an action or a happening. In the sentence *I ate the cake* the verb is 'ate'. These are sometimes referred to as 'doing' words.

Adjective

A word that modifies a noun. In the phrase *the little boat* the adjective 'little' describes the noun 'boat'.

Adverb
A word that modifies a verb. In the phrase *he walked slowly* the adverb is 'slowly'.

Preposition
A word or phrase that shows the relationship of one thing to another. In the phrase *the house beside the sea* the preposition 'beside' places the two nouns in relation to each other.

Conjunction
A word or phrase that joins other words and phrases. A simple example is the word 'and' that joins nouns in *Snow White and Doc and Sneezy*.

Determiner
Determiners appear before nouns and denote whether the noun is specific (*give me the book*) or not (*give me a book*). Note that 'the' (definite article) and 'a' or 'an' (indefinite articles) are the most common types of determiner.

Interjection
A word or phrase expressing or exclaiming an emotion, such as 'Oh!' and 'Aaargh!'.
The various word types can be found in the following example sentences:

Yeow!	I	hit	my	head	on	the	door.
Interjection	Pronoun	Verb	Pronoun	Noun	Preposition	Article	Noun
Amir	sadly	lost	his	bus fare	down	the	drain.
Noun	Adverb	Verb	Pronoun	Noun	Preposition	Article	Noun
Give	Jan	a	good	book	for	her	birthday.
Verb	Noun	Article	Adjective	Noun	Conjunction	Pronoun	Noun

Grammar and Punctuation Years 1 and 2 focuses on nouns, verbs, adjectives and conjunctions. The pages that follow provide more information on these word classes.

Nouns
There are four types of noun in English.

Common nouns are general names for things. For example, in the sentence *I fed the dog*, the noun 'dog' could be used to refer to any dog, not to a specific one. Other examples include 'boy', 'country', 'book', 'apple'.

Proper nouns are the specific names given to identify things or people. In a phrase like *Sam is my dog* the word 'dog' is the common noun but 'Sam' is a proper noun because it refers to and identifies a specific dog. Other examples include 'Wales' and 'Amazing Grace'.

Collective nouns refer to a group of things together, such as 'a flock (of sheep)' or 'a bunch (of bananas)'.

Abstract nouns refer to things that are not concrete, such as an action, a concept, an event, quality or state. Examples are 'happiness', 'anger' and 'joke'.

Nouns can be singular or plural. To change a singular to a plural the usual rule is to add 's'. There are some other rules to bear in mind, however:

If the singular ends in:	Rule	Example
'y' after a consonant	Remove 'y', add 'ies'	party → parties
'y' after a vowel	add 's'	donkey → donkeys
'o' after a consonant	add 'es'	potato → potatoes
'o' after a vowel	add 's'	video → videos
an 's' sound such as 's', 'sh', 'x', 'z'	add 'es'	kiss → kisses dish → dishes
a 'ch' sound such as 'ch' or 'tch'	add 'es'	watch → watches church → churches

Verbs

The **tense** of a verb places a happening in time. The main three tenses are the present and past.

English does not have a discrete future tense. It is made in a compound form using a present tense ('I will', 'I shall' and so on) and an infinitive (for example *I will go to the shops*).

The regular past tense is formed by the addition of the suffix 'ed', although some of the most common verbs in English have irregular past tenses.

Present tense (happening now)	Past tense (happened in past)	Future (to happen in future)
am	was	will be
say	said	will say
find	found	shall find
kick	kicked	shall kick

Adjectives

The main functions of adjectives are to define quality or quantity. Examples of the use of descriptions of quality include: 'good story', 'sad day' and 'stupid dog'. Examples of the use of descriptions of quantity include 'some stories', 'ten days' and 'many dogs'.

Adjectives can appear in one of three different degrees of intensity. The regular comparative is formed by the addition of the suffix 'er' to shorter words and 'more' to longer words (kind/kinder, beautiful/more beautiful). The regular superlative is formed by the addition of the suffix 'est' to shorter words and 'most' to longer words. Note, however, that some common adjectives have irregular comparatives and superlatives.

Nominative	Comparative	Superlative
big fast bad good far	bigger faster worse better farther/further	biggest fastest worst best farthest/furthest

Conjunctions

Conjunctions are words or phrases that join words or clauses in one of four ways.

Type of conjunction	Nature of conjunction	Example
Addition	One or more things together	We had our tea **and** went out to play. Snow White **and** Doc **and** Sneezy **and** Sleepy
Opposition	One or more things in opposition	I like coffee **but** my brother hates it.
Time	One or more things connected temporally	Sobia had her tea **then** went out to play.
Cause	One or more things causing or caused by another	We got lost **because** we had the wrong map.

3. Understanding sentences

Types of sentence

The four main types of sentence are declarative, interrogative, imperative and exclamatory. The function of a sentence has an effect upon the word order; imperatives, for example, generally begin with a verb.

Sentence type	Definition	Examples
Declarative	Makes a statement	The house is down the lane. Joe rode the bike.
Interrogative	Asks a question	Where is the house? What is Joe doing?
Imperative	Issues a command or direction	Turn left at the traffic lights. Get on your bike!
Exclamatory	Issues an interjection	Wow, what a mess! Oh no!

4. Punctuation

Punctuation provides marks within sentences that guide the reader, indicating when to pause, when something is being quoted and so on.

Punctuation at work

Punctuation mark	Uses	Examples
A	**Capital letter** 1. Starts a sentence. 2. Indicates proper nouns. 3. Emphasises certain words.	1. All I want is cake. 2. You can call me Al. 3. I want it TOMORROW!
.	**Full stop** Ends sentences that are not questions or exclamations.	This is a sentence.
?	**Question mark** Ends a sentence that is a question.	Is this a question?
!	**Exclamation mark** Ends a sentence that is an exclamation.	Don't do that!
" "	**Inverted commas (or quotation/ speech marks)** Encloses direct speech.	"Help me," the man yelled.
,	**Comma** 1. Places a pause between clauses within a sentence. 2. Separates items in a list. 3. Separates adjectives in a series. 4. Completely encloses clauses inserted in a sentence. 5. Marks speech from words denoting who said them.	1. We were late, although it didn't matter. 2. You will need eggs, butter and flour. 3. I wore a long, green, frilly skirt. 4. We were, after we had rushed to get there, late for the film. 5. 'Thank you,' I said.
'	**Apostrophe of possession** Denotes the ownership of one thing by another.	This is Mona's scarf. These are the teachers' books.
'	**Apostrophe of contraction** Shows the omission of a letter(s) when two (or occasionally more) words are contracted.	Don't walk on the grass.